Practical
Dinghy Cruiser

Paul Constantine

Distributed. Moonshine Publications.
Printed. Tawny Press

© Paul Constantine. 2013
Distributed in the UK by
Moonshine Publications
Woodbridge, Suffolk.
14 / IP12 4EU.

First Edition 2010. Leiston Press.
Second   2013. Tawny Press
4, Perry Road, Witham,
Essex. CM8 3YZ

ISBN – 978-0-9572161-1-2

A CIP catalogue record for this book is available from the British Library.

Wonderful, wonderful illustrations by David Summerville.

Edited. Typeset & Design. Paul Constantine & Annie Barnes
Distributed.   www.moonshinepublications.co.uk.

Front Cover. Wayfarer 'Outlander' Ian and William Hyton.
Thanks to Liz Baker and Keith Muscott.
Inside Cover. Photo Roger Barnes.

Back Cover pictures from. Dick Houghton.
Dad and son Arran. Alastair Law.
The family with mum's boat.
(Alison's Mirror is light enough to manoeuvre on land by herself.)
DCA boats sail in company.

Proofreading. By the late Ted Jones.
'Advice from a lifetime's experience in small boats.'

Thanks too to Alison, my wife. I am most grateful to you both.

Photographs.
Liz Baker, Roger Barnes, Colin Bell, Dick Houghton, John Hughes, Dave Jennings, Alastair Law, Keith Muscott, Chris Perkins, George Strube, Chris Waite, Ed Wingfield, Small Craft Advisor.

With special thanks to the DCA members and others who have allowed their material to be referenced or included. There are so many more members with a wealth of ideas and experiences that I would have loved to have listed here. It is just chance that these were the people who happened to be included.
My apologies to those that I have missed.

Joan Abrams, John Baden, Bill Bailey, Renee & Jim Bailey, Liz Baker, Alan Barker, Roger Barnes, Colin Bell, Peter Bick, Steve Bradwell A. Campbell, Hugh Clay, Derrick Cobden, Matthew Cunningham, John Deacon, Roy Downes, Margaret Dye, Archie Campbell, Eric Coleman, Martin Cooperman, John Deacon, Colin Firth, David Fraser, Duncan Gilchrist, I. A. Gill, Alan Glanville, Roger Gomm, John Gray, David Hall, Derek Harvey, Doug Heslop, Keith Holdsworth, Dick Houghton, John Huntingford, Mike Jackson, Bill Jones, David Jones, Ted Jones, Anne & Dennis Kell, Alastair Law, John Lidstone, Bill Lingsley, Cliff Martin, Brian McClellan, David McClellan, Peter and Averil Merrin, Mukti Mitchell, Howard Morgan, Dave Morl, Keith Muscott, Brian Naylor, David Platten, P. Philpott John Perry & Josephine, George Saffrey, Bill Serjeant, L.J. Shields, Anthony Sluce, Charles Stock, David Sumner, Chris Waite, Mike Williams, Ed Wingfield, Len Wingfield, Peter Whyman.

CONTENTS.

Reefed sailing. Heavy Weather. Storm mainsail. Light wind sailing. Bowsprit. Roller Headsail, Tube, Drum (luff tension, bearings, planning, sail). Sail area / Performance. Bailing. Foredeck spray deflector. Diaphragm Pump. Stopping the boat. Anchoring. Some useful tips. Beaching. Ballasted Boats. Fender / Rollers. Marina mooring. Moorings. Shelter. The Tent. The Specification. Fabrication. The Bow Cuddy. The main tent canopy. Tent poles. Lifejacket in bed? Renee & Jim Bailey lazy sailing.

1.

Discovering
the
Dinghy Cruiser.

DCA Quotes.

(About the DCA.) *'Informed, friendly, only minimally organised, an Association for individuals who meet from time to time, before going their own ways again.'*

Joan Abrams.

1.
Practical Dinghy Cruiser.

Who Cruises? What is cruising?

Let me show you just a few brief 'snapshots' of the hundreds, nay, thousands of dinghy cruising experiences, so that you will begin to appreciate how far these questions can take us.

<u>Liz Baker & John Quantrell sail her 12' 9" x 5' 6" Mayfly dinghy</u>
<u>'Black Swan' to Fingal's Cave on Staffa sailing from Iona 123/09</u>
At 09.00am Staffa again disappeared into the mist ... At 09.30 it loomed out of the mist fine on the port bow and very close ... At 09.45 we arrived bang on our ETA and hove-to off the cave entrance to eat a bannock for breakfast. Staffa looked dark and awesome in the mist, like a huge and slightly lopsided organ. Our early arrival had been calculated to give us time to see the island before the tourist boats arrived ...

John was keen to take 'Black Swan' into the cave. I thought it was too rough. The wind had increased to F4 and quite a swell was running. We investigated a landing ... but there was a real danger of being pounded against the rocks. Then we lowered sail and rowed about, getting the feel for rowing in the swell ... Eventually John convinced me that he could safely row into the cave. The ceiling is very high so there were no fears for the mast, but the channel is too narrow for turning. We entered stern first, John skilfully negotiating the rocks at the entrance. Apparently when it is calm one can land on a beach at the head of the cave, but today we didn't dare go in so far. John kept 'Black Swan' as steady as possible as we surged back and forth about 10ft. in the swell, while I stood by the mast taking photos ... When we emerged, John rowing and myself by the mast shouting directions there was the first tourist boat hove-to outside, its passengers lining the rail, cameras at the ready. We waved and they all cheered. They were clearly astonished at our sudden appearance.

We did eventually land in a more sheltered bay ... on a large slab of rock rather like a stone jetty ... I found the walking route into the cave far more frightening than going in by boat. By now the weather was most unpleasant with a heavy drizzle falling which made the rocks very slippery for walking on in wellies. On one of the wider stretches of hexagonal pavement I fell flat on my back. The path into the cave is very narrow and definitely not for high-heeled shoes or the faint hearted ... Apparently there is a button to press, which will play Mendelssohn's Fingal's Cave Overture, but we didn't know that ... When I'd penetrated as far as I dared and John was back in the entrance, I decided to try the acoustics so sang a couple of verses of 'Eternal Father, Strong to Save' – it seemed appropriate somehow! My voice sounded squeaky and inadequate in that vast chasm. "How was that?" I asked John later, expecting his usual ribald comment about my singing. "Terrific. It sounded like a whole choir in there."

Note. An explanation of any unusual numbers such as 123/09 or 89/20 will be found on page 19 and final page.

Hugh Clay translates. Drifting on Lake Vattern, Sweden. 89/20.
Open 17ft double ender.

When we had been half an hour absolutely still in the sweltering heat, I stripped off and began rowing towards an idyllic and deserted little bay with a superb beach about two miles away. As we approached I spotted notices at the top of the beach. So as we grounded, I took the dictionary and trotted up the beach, still naked. There I stood working my way slowly through the notice. 'Beware!' it said, 'Danger to life beyond this point from military exercises.' But they saved the biggest surprise to the end. 'We ...are watching ... you with closed-circuit television.' I closed the dictionary, returned to 'Eel' and we rowed out of the bay in dignified haste.

Bill Lingsley and Donald find adventure,
Hired Drascombe Lugger, Loch Lomond. 78/19

This, our first island of the holiday, was superb. We decided to walk across it and find the lily inlet and, whilst we did this we were impressed with the solitude. Memories of 'Treasure Island' flooded back and we decided that 'Lily Inlet' was an excellent name for that part of the island. With a singular lack of originality I led Donald up 'Spyglass Hill' and halfway up it we found a hole, which obviously contained the Silver treasure. By now we were hot on the track of the gold and expecting to meet Long John Silver at any moment. I am convinced that we would have found it had not pangs of hunger of gigantic proportions forced us to return to the lugger. After dinner, as twilight deepened, we constructed a fire of some of the old branches which lie everywhere in profusion, and even later sat in the flickering darkness eating potatoes baked in the hot embers. It had been a truly memorable day.

Bill Bailey goes to the Pub. 127/09. 17ft. Inflatable Catamaran.

A wall of white ahead, a breeze, we vanish, swallowed up. The world shrinks in, cold, dank, and grey. Puffs and lulls and drizzle all the day. 135 magnetic – just do it. The Point of Sleat. Land, sea and sky slate-grey. A lift, it's filling, we're away. Cold boned, stiff, rain driven we round the corner to the anchorage. The run turns into a smoking reach in the squall, tearing through the moorings. Found eyes peering from within warm ketches. Hard on the wind now, two quick tacks. "Over there – that little patch by the quay." As we come tearing in, the hotel bar in front empties. They can't believe their eyes. "What sort of fools? – wouldn't put a dog out ...Like drowned rats" We let fly and run straight up on the sand. Two heaves, then straight into the bar ahead. " Have you anything hot? And two large malts as well, please." Puddles grow on the floor – amused smiles all around. The hotel Eilean Iarmain – hospitable, welcoming and warm.

John Gray meets show-offs. Mirror dinghy. Wales. 102/22

A school of porpoises! As I watched I could see from the surface splashes that the school was heading to cross our course. Soon 'Little Mischief' was in the middle of them, playfully jumping right out of the water, singly, in twos and threes. On both sides I saw some swim up to us a few feet below the surface, then turn away. The finale to the show came, and it _was_ a finale, because afterwards I saw only the occasional splash as they moved away, when four porpoises leapt out of the water about 10 yds. off our port bow, in close line abreast on our heading. Must be real show-offs to do that when they know someone is looking. To me it was a new and wonderful experience. Made me feel like a real blue water sailor.

I.A. Gill and Vic cross the Channel (before the use of GPS.). 'Beachcomber' Open dinghy, No engine. Dungeness beach. 84/17

Wind, they said, WSW about 15 knots.
"Vic," I said, running back, "we're off."
Reaching in a F4 wind we should make a good crossing. We launched 'Beachcomber', stowed the gear and were clear of the point by 12.30pm, a bit late to start off but we had ten hours of daylight before us and we had had a good rest.

Whilst still at anchor off the beach I had looked at the chart and set a compass course for Boulogne entrance, distance about 26 miles. The actual crossing was very enjoyable and more or less uneventful. The seas were still plenty big enough but not uncomfortable. We sailed with the centreplate right up so that 'Beachcomber' slid over the beam seas rather than trying to slice through them, thus we enjoyed a dry ride. This caused me to wonder if I had allowed enough for leeway. When a feminine looking French buoy came in sight, we found that our course took us within a few yards of it. It seemed to me that we were making too much easting. I preferred to arrive too far west of Boulogne, upwind of it, than arrive too far to the east and have to beat upwind to make the harbour. I altered course more to the south, the broad reach now became a close reach, the plate was lowered a little, spray began to come on board and the foredeck got wet for the first time that day. 16.30 hrs. We sighted land, visibility wasn't good but we took it to be Cape Gris Nez. In time we began to identify some of the shore marks with the aid of the chart. It soon became evident that we were two or three miles too far to the west. Altering course, plate up, we began to run down to Boulogne breakwater, 'Beachcomber' once again surfing. It was 19.30 when we passed between the piers, 'Q' signal flying.

In the lee of the railway station and quay there was no wind. The glory of sailing into the harbour had left us and we were now an insignificant rowing boat looking for a berth.

John Gray, smuggler? Mirror dinghy. Wales. 102/23

After chatting for a while to a Mirror owner on holiday without his boat, my new friend collected a few healthy looking men from the beach and they pulled 'Little Mischief' over a bank of shingle into a pool which was fed from a small stream running down the valley, so it didn't dry out.

I put the tent up and prepared to spend the night there. About 18.30 when most of the holiday makers had gone, I was making the evening meal, looking over the stern through the open tent, when I saw the local bobby coming down the shingle. No hat; hands in pockets; so I knew it couldn't be serious. As we were floating in the pool he couldn't come right up to the boat, but called across asking in Welsh if I spoke Welsh. I don't, but after 30 years in Wales I'd heard the question enough times to know what he was saying. "No," I replied, "I'm Scottish." I always find it best to let them know I might be a foreigner, but at least a fellow Celt and not

English. "Scottish." he said, rolling the word around his mouth as though testing it. After a few questions on what I was doing and proposed to do, he then explained in a rather embarrassed way that they'd had a phone call from someone who'd heard the recent reports of some arrests about 30 miles to the south, a few days before, for drug smuggling from a small boat. Their informant thought that I looked suspicious by appearing in that small cove in a small boat. After putting down my name and address in his little book, he wished me a friendly goodnight and wandered back up the shingle.

Who Cruises? What is cruising? Were the original questions and I am hoping that by now you may be seeing that there are almost limitless possibilities. These 'snapshots' cover widely separated locations in different countries, at sea and inland, in a variety of craft whose only common denominator is that they are small boats, sometimes very small. They are dinghies. And what of the people?

Well all types. It can be said that there are two kinds of dinghy sailor the racer and the cruiser. No matter which kind of sailing is adopted, the choice of boat that they use will be of the utmost importance to them. 'Cruising' in sailing has often been a word applied to all those who go afloat under sail, but who do not race. It includes aimless drifting and gentle pottering as well as folks who just sail to enjoy the sensation of moving around on the water in a boat. 'Cruising' can also have another sense that is most frequently used when related to yachts, meaning 'living aboard' the boat, exploring or travelling to different locations. This is the kind of sailing described in this book, 'living' aboard a dinghy and using it as a means of getting from one place to another. We might say 'travelling and camping' in a dinghy. This kind of cruising appears to be relatively rare in dinghies as most people regard them as being too small to carry the creature comforts of life, probably too open to the elements and the exposure of their occupants, for extended periods of time. But all is not as it may seem.

The number of sailors who pursue this activity is limited compared to the racing fraternity, but almost by definition, because the dinghy cruisers are in a minority, they are often very dedicated individualists. Racing needs numbers of people, needs them to agree on complex rules. Success in racing needs a competitive nature, ambition to win and an ability to use the boat as a functional machine, tuned to its maximum efficiency. People who cruise aboard dinghies do not necessarily need others sailing alongside them, they make up their own rules and usually they are willing to trade maximum efficiency for a degree of comfort. They have the time to become more emotionally involved with their boat, its surroundings and the activity, because they 'live' in the situation, sometimes for several days and nights at a time, rather than briefly packing their experience into one hectic section of part of a day, as a 'racer' might do.

It is said that you know if you are this kind of a 'cruiser', but whilst you might know it, there is a chance that you may not know how to do it, even if you have a boat. Individual dinghy cruisers are thinly spread and rarely congregate. You can sail past them without knowing that they are engaged in cruising, but there are more of them about than many people suspect. I will return to the dinghy cruisers whose 'snapshots' you have seen to explain more, later.

Can I do it?

If you have an inclination to join their ranks how do you find out about dinghy cruisers? Where should you go and what should you do? How can you gain experience? What can you do to experience cruising, if you don't have a boat? What is a suitable boat? What work needs to be done to make a boat suitable for cruising? Do you have the practical skills? Do you have the finance? Hopefully you are about to find out, but a small word of warning. If you feel inclined to be a dinghy cruiser, please don't be put off by anything that you read in this book. When all that could be done is slowly revealed to you; when several scary tales are told, it can appear to be overwhelming. The cautionary tales will be mainly my practical experiences, but remember that I did not do these things all at one time. It took me years of stumbling around and gradually experimenting and evolving. There is no hurry. The concept is to have some fun along the way, in finding a boat, then adding, experimenting, and modifying your ideas and equipment to make up a cruising unit that does what you want it to do in your own way.

What follows should allow you to 'convert' in the philosophical sense as well as 'practically converting' any suitable craft that you might have or might acquire, in order to make your kind of cruising possible for you. The challenges of the journey can equal or surpass the satisfaction of arriving.

What this book doesn't do.

It doesn't teach you to sail. I will use and sometimes explain some nautical terms, but to cruise safely you should already be able to sail. If you are a non-sailor, find a way to learn properly. This means getting instruction from a competent person, using the right equipment and sailing in a safe place, preferably non-tidal water to begin with. (See advice at end of book.) This book is not intending to instruct about sailing, so each and every person must satisfy themselves about the safety of their own activities as well as the durability of any equipment they may use or fabricate for themselves. Everything that follows attempts to encourage individuals to take responsibility for their own actions, being mindful of their own safety and that of others too.

Before going further. Two essential starting points.
Do you want to read <u>another</u> book about Dinghy Cruising?
Probably the best one is (early version) ISBN 0-7136-3453-7:
'Dinghy Cruising' The Enjoyment of Wandering Afloat.
by Margaret Dye, published by Adlard Coles (now in later editions) it covers the subject comprehensively and it will give you a very good idea of what is involved. Incidentally, Margaret's late husband Frank Dye is probably the most widely known of dinghy cruisers and he has a number of publications to look out for too. Frank and Margaret have been ordinary members of the D.C.A

Do you want a Website contact?
Try **www.dinghycruising.org.uk**
This is the contact for the Dinghy Cruising Association.
(also) :http://groups.yahoo.com/group/**openboat/**
Who is/are the Dinghy Cruising Association?
It is more or less what it says in its title. It is a group of people, all individuals and volunteers who cruise in all kinds of dinghies and as a result they have a loose association with each other, as like-minded people. There are no 'headquarter buildings' and few regular meeting places so this may seem a like a vague kind of organisation to a newcomer, but for anybody wishing to become involved in dinghy cruising it could well provide the key. The <u>DCA publications are a fundamental resource for readers of this book,</u> because they will provide so much extra background information if it is required. You will see as we go along that, in many ways, this book is almost an advert for the DCA. However, it has not been produced by the Association, but by an individual, appreciative member who is grateful to other members for allowing their work to be quoted or referred to. The 'snapshots' that you read at the beginning came from members accounts of their cruising activities.

What does the DCA do?

You can get hold of a little leaflet about the DCA by contacting the Secretary through their website and it will tell you that since it started in 1955 the organisation has acted as a pool for sharing information about dinghy cruising. To this end it can put you in touch, through its membership, with someone who dinghy cruises and who probably lives near to you. It has people who are ready to assist with technical advice if needed and it can tell you about sailing meetings that will happen in your area (Britain). Most significant of all, it is driven by its members who publish a quarterly Bulletin that is composed of accounts of cruises, boats and equipment. You have already seen brief 'snapshot' examples.

It will be appreciated that well over 50 years of Bulletins represents an enormous body of knowledge about dinghy cruising and it is probably the largest (and best?) general fund of information that can be accessed anywhere, on this subject.

How can I access the information?

Membership fees are minimal and might be thought of as a very modest subscription to a specialist quarterly magazine. Check them on the website. It is cheap because those who run it are unpaid. Members seeking information contact the DCA Librarian who can supply an index for the bulletins. This index is large, running to well over 100 pages. The secretary can also supply an index of sailing related books, charts, publications etc. that the Association possesses and loans out to its members who simply pay postage; email is also used. Almost anything that you may wish to read on sailing cruising will be here. (See note at end of book)

If all that anyone wishes to know about dinghy cruising is in the DCA information store, what is this book about?

It is about boats and an individual who some years ago may have been in a similar situation to yourself, in possessing some sailing experience, in wishing to try cruising in a dinghy, but who knew nobody to ask about it, and did not know what would be involved. What follows is an outline of the path taken from this starting point and of the decisions that were taken along the way. It has a particular emphasis on the practical aspects of fitting out a boat for dinghy cruising, of inventing pieces of equipment and making them from simple, low cost materials. You may follow if you wish and hopefully avoid some of the mistakes. If you should decide to sail a similar track, it is hoped that you will not slavishly copy everything, but make your own decisions to go and do it your own way.

9

<u>Some Cruising Principles.</u>

What's it about? (Cruising Concept)

I once heard a sailor say, "It's a lovely day. I'd like to go sailing but there isn't a race on." If you couldn't go sailing because there wasn't a race on, then maybe this is not for you? This book is more about a kind of cruising journey.

I also once heard a cruising story of a yacht crew sailing from Scandinavia. They suffered the hardship of running out of drinking water on their boat when crossing the North Sea to England. The incident came about because one of the children on board left the tap running in the bathroom after cleaning their teeth. Nobody noticed until the water was gone. They managed the rest of the journey on the contents of the drinks cabinet and by using one of the engines to shorten the journey time. If this kind of luxury living is your idea of cruising, then be prepared for the concept of hardship to be redefined.

Dinghy cruising is more suited to people who don't mind camping, are prepared to get a bit damp from time to time and who can enjoy the experience of sailing small boats even if they are going slowly or even not going at all. The idea is to go camping by boat so as to get that one step nearer to elemental nature and therefore, briefly, to get that one step further away from our modern industrial world with its commonplace luxuries.

Sailing as a sport has several branches. There are branches on branches, twigs on branches and twigs on twigs. There's no one way to do it, so the diversity of dinghy cruisers is as wide as with any other part of the sport.

A group of dinghy cruisers prepare their boats.

Where to begin?

Anyone who has had the idea of dinghy cruising and who wishes to put it into practice must first decide what kind of cruising and therefore what kind of a boat is right for them. Selecting the boat is the biggest single problem and if you have no experience, how can you possibly make a start? One way is to 'read and learn' (Margaret Dye's book and the DCA) then to think about everything in theory before looking to buy a suitable boat. Other people may already be in possession of their own boat and they will have to evaluate it for its potential to be used for cruising. Anyone owning a boat already would probably begin with considering if it has the space on board and is sufficiently robust for what it is required to do. Whether you are a complete outsider or whether you have some experience, you still have to work out what will suit you. What suits you, may not necessarily suit everyone else, so what you intend to undertake may involve you in NOT following well-tried ways, but in developing ways for yourself. So what stage are you at now? Let's find out.

The Questionnaire.

The following questions are intended to help you to try to understand what your concept of dinghy cruising might be. Settling on some intentions can begin to paint the picture for you. Before going further you should:

Get a piece of paper and record your answers

honestly for yourself, NOW, before your mind gets cluttered with all that will comes afterwards. At this moment your mind could be like a blank piece of paper, but deep down you may have some vague 'ideas'. What is it that is attracting you to the idea of dinghy cruising? It might be useful to find a few answers. There are no 'right' answers. It's not that kind of a quiz. If you don't know an answer just write what YOU think at present. You will be able to look back later and change your decisions if you wish, but it is important to record your present thoughts. My suggestions are only there to help you make a start. Don't skip over this. Do it!
Go slowly and think about it.

Now ... Pencil and Paper at the ready?

Practical Dinghy Cruiser

A Personal Questionnaire.
Where are you going to sail?
On reservoirs and lakes?
On rivers and estuaries?
Out at sea?
At home locally, or abroad?
Another location?

You will understand with only a little thought that your boat will have to be tougher as you move from inland waters to tidal waters and the sea. Your choices should also be shaped by the amount of previous experience that you have already.

How will you sail?
In one place from a home base?
By traveling to different locations?
Will you get the boat there under sail?
Or by road?

This raises the issues of mooring on the water or berthing ashore and whether you are hoping to trail, then launch and recover the boat. Where will you store the boat for sailing? Out of season? Where will you store its road trailer?

How many people will you usually have on board?
Will you usually be singlehanded? Or with crew?
What will their age, experience, relationship and gender be?

Whilst all the questions so far have in some way related to the size of the boat, this question in particular, begins to determine minimum sizes. Your responsibility for safety, as a skipper, is also an issue. Cruising can mean living closely with other people. This is a major addition to the relatively simple process of sailing.

Why would you choose to dinghy cruise?
You can't afford any other method of cruising?
You like the mobility it affords?
You want to learn to cruise?
You're planning to test the limits of your own endurance with extended journeys in close to life-threatening conditions?
You wish to go somewhere quiet, to get away from it all?
Other reasons? (Adventure. Outlet for practical skills. Etc.)

These questions and thoughts are tied to all the previous ones. They are just some of the basic questions that might be addressed right at the beginning. I can't help you with the answers. Only you know what they are.

Most people rarely analyse their intentions in the early stages of an activity, they tend just to drift along reacting to the circumstances that they find themselves in. In this sport (some call it a way of life) there are fundamental differences in the equipment required between one kind of cruising and another, particularly as the boats are so small they tend to determine the limits of what is possible. A boat that is going to be daysailed in fresh water is probably not going to be equipped like another one which is used for extended offshore journeys. If you think that you know in which direction you will be heading you can get the basic decisions correct from the beginning rather than having to re-think them later, which can prove to be expensive.

Have you learned anything about your sailing goals from the questions? Will you be able to identify which branch (or which twig) of sailing might interest you the most? Is your intention at this moment to team up with a friend and sail on a local lake, or do you feel you would like to involve your family in being on the water instead of just you racing alone all the time? Are you fed up with your local water and do you intend to tow the boat to a new location? Each and every person has his or her own motivation. Look at the questions and turn the answers over in your mind until you begin to understand what you really want to do; your requirement may be unique. A DCA member David Hall wrote about his experiences 197/36 (*these numbers are explained on page 19*) under a heading 'How a small boat on a lake brings great peace of mind.' In it he wrote *'I decided to spend every Tuesday night out on the water ... my work finished late on a Tuesday ... I had been in the habit of driving home just to sleep, have breakfast and return.'* He decided not to go home but to overnight on his boat, so he would launch it and sail on 'his' lake to various places to enjoy the solitude or the scenery. He says *'My Tuesday nights were neither about sailing nor exploring. They were just about being there.'* Whilst he enjoyed being alone, he is not alone in being involved in this kind of individual activity.

2.

About Boats.

DCA Quotes.

'I began without money, boat or commitments.
That left me little choice but to earn money, buy a boat and go off
sailing.'
Hugh Clay.

2.
About Boats.
Some things you need to know.

The Dinghy.

The boat that is used will be the single most important piece of equipment so it is essential for us to spend some time discussing it and trying to understand the advantages and disadvantages that will follow from the choice of craft. First we will begin with a rather surprising question.

What is a dinghy?

With your questionnaire answers in mind we should perhaps take a look at the kind of craft that is under consideration here. There are various forms of craft called a 'dinghy' but for the purpose of my writing I have chosen to deal with boats that are essentially **open dayboats** and in the main **unballasted**. They have various levels of decking and may use a little cuddy (simple small cabin) forward.

Within the Dinghy Cruising Association there are a number of small cruisers (Sunspot 15, Skipper 17/ Eagle 525, etc.) that are sometimes referred to as 'pocket cruisers', or 'dinghies-with-lids'. Sailing on these craft is not quite the same as pure 'open dinghy' cruising (as we shall see later) but nevertheless the two types do mix well and share many similarities. This type of craft may be more

Ted Jones' Sunspot, 'The Genie'

suitable for you than being out in an open boat.

Fundamental Factors.

I cannot say where your answers might be leading you. However, whatever the answers are, the qualities of any boat will be shaped by certain fundamentals and I am going to outline four interrelated factors at this point. I warn you that parts of this will sound quite technical, but it is important to appreciate these factors from an early stage. (*The section about weight is very detailed for later reference, so I* suggest that you might skip over the statistics and come back to *them later if you want them for comparison.)* These very important factors are linked to any boat being evaluated in this size range. The first element that needs to be investigated further is **'weight'**. As I just warned, we are going to have to get rather technical by looking at this and other differences between craft.

Weight and performance.

The way that a boat responds to the elements, its performance, will be governed by many factors, but these first two are probably the primary ones. (See S.A./Displacement ratios Martin Corrick 211/15) **Weight** and **Sail area.**

Evaluating the performance of boats.

You can think of the sails as the 'engine' or the 'power unit', of the boat. Some careful consideration will show that a heavier boat will need more sail area if it is to perform in a similar way to a lighter boat. In other words a boat weighing 150 kg being pushed along by 100 sq ft of sail will go faster than a boat weighing 200kg with the same sail area, all other things being equal. On the other hand, speed may not be the prime requirement. The heavier boat would be more stable and possibly more comfortable than the lighter craft. So what kind of performance will you require, one with speed or one with comfort? Or some kind of blend of the two?

Weight.

I am going to dig a little deeper here into the problems of weight and give some approximate weights for my boat (I'll explain what type it is in a moment) to provide some comparisons that you may find useful at a later stage, because as I have already indicated, weight is so very important as one of the primary factors in determining performance. The hull weight rarely represents the total all-up weight of the craft and there are choices to be made about weight even on two similar boats within the same class. For example, my old boat has wooden spars whilst later craft in the same class replaced them with aluminium. It will be seen that updating the mast would save 1.25 kg where is matters most, up aloft. This amount of weight saving may not appear to be important, but as you will see the weight all adds up and if you do not want it to become excessive you must evaluate it in the search for weight saving. My old fashioned floorboards weigh 15kgs in total, but they are low down, thus adding to stability; they secure other items in place (anchor, water etc) and are converted to make my bed. How would they compare with flooring systems used in later models such as plywood panels?

The general weights that follow will be of interest. Note **hull weight**. (*Skip to* 'The most immediate effect of' *next page, if you wish.*)
My basic hull.   115 kg (253lbs)   (About 18 stones)

Mast and rigging	5 kg	Gaff 3.75 kg.	Total = 8.75 kg.

(*Aluminium mast and rig = 7.5 kg.*)

Oars 2kgs. each	4.0 kg	Aft Floorboards 3.5 kg each	7.0kg
Wooden Boom	2.25 kg	Fwd Floorboards 4.0kg each	8.0kg
Plywood C/board	3.5 kg	Bilge pump/holder	2.0 kg
Mainsheet + blocks	1.0 kg	Main and Jib + sheet	2.75 kg
Anchor reel + warp	1.0 kg	5lb CQR/3.6m,12ft chain	4.25 kg
Rudder	3.5 kg	Tiller + Extension	1.0 kg
Stern scissor poles	2.25 kg	All poles + Ensign staff	1.25 kg
Storm main kit	1.25 kg	Bowsprit/Reacher + lines	2.0 kg
Inflatable roller	1.5 kg	Big fender + lines (roller)	2.5 kg
Tent canopy	5.0 kg	Toilet seat + box/spares	2.0 kg
Warps + lines	1.5 kg	Plast. locker box some kit	1.25 kg
Launch trolley	17.0 kg	Jockey wheel	3.75 kg

The thwart from a modern inflatable, that might do the same task as the inflatable roller weighs only 500gms. It can be seen that the inflatable roller (used as additional buoyancy) and the large fender also used as a boat roller for moving the boat on land, together weigh 4.0 kg, which is significant. If I replaced them with two thwart bags, then I could save 3 kg of weight. This is a good saving and demonstrates how it might pay off to constantly reassess the boat and its equipment. It may not be the 'grand' change of the mast that saves the most weight; it might be the apparently insignificant substitution of one kind of buoyancy device for another that will make the difference. Will I change my wooden spars to aluminium and save 1.25 kg in weight? No, because it will fundamentally alter the boat's appearance and I like the way she looks, as she is. Will I change the roller and fender? I'll have to think about that. Inflatable thwarts are expensive. Maybe I'll 'retire' the old roller and keep the fender? This is the way that one uses the knowledge about weight and performance. Some people constantly pare down weight, and some feel that it's not too critical. Racing sailors will be weighing gear in grams and it is interesting to see that many gear manufacturers now include the weight of pieces of equipment on the packaging. Read 'Weight Watching' Roy Downes 187/26. One of my experienced teenage sons went for a trial ride in a modern racing dinghy. He almost capsized it as he stepped aboard, it was so unstable and its helmsman had to take immediate action to keep it upright. They had an exhilarating sail and came back happy but exhausted. It is 'horses for courses' and this boat would not have made a comfortable 'live-aboard' cruising dinghy. Whatever you decide, you should always be aware of weight and understand its effect on what you are trying to do.

The most immediate effect of weight is felt when you come to launch or recover the boat on a sloping slipway or try to return it to the water across soft ground. The weight list above relates mainly to the boat and its functioning gear, the stuff that's always on it. This is a modest sized craft and probably being cruised by a single person yet the hull weighs 115 kg and its gear about 70 kg. When it is on its launching trolley it will be around 205 kg (451lbs) and then the personal cruising gear (water, food, bedding, utensils, clothes etc.) goes aboard. This is serious weight.

I might digress slightly here to say that technology has now advanced to a point where I feel that it is possible to design a roomy, stable boat with all its equipment, including its tent, at half of this total weight or even less, but it will be an extremely difficult design challenge, exploiting the latest materials and manufacturing techniques, costing real money, as buying 'lightness' is expensive.
Two more very important factors are:
The wetted surface area (How much of the boat is touching the water and being 'dragged' through it).
The stiffness of the boat (How easily the boat leans over when a gust of wind hits the sail). These factors tend to relate to the 'size' of the boat. One priority might be how much space there is inside the boat, but the wider and fatter a boat becomes (thus creating internal space) the more probable it is, that it has more of its outside surface pushing down into the water, creating drag to slow it. There may be an advantage in having a wide boat, as it will not heel over as quickly as a narrow craft when pressed over by a gust. As it is broader, it will stand more upright for longer, thus extracting more power from the wind. If broadness can be achieved without too much added weight then it will begin to markedly improve the speed of the craft. This is an area exploited by multihulls that make themselves wide, but without extra weight and drag.

A bit about Dimensions.
To gauge the likely performance of boats one needs to study the

basic dimensions and learn to relate them to each other. This may never give an absolutely true picture but it will allow a rough idea to be formed in the mind. It is useful to have one craft whose performance is known to you, so that you can use it as a 'yardstick' to measure other craft. Perhaps I should I introduce you to my own dinghy-cruising boat, which is a Torch class. This is NOT a widely known design, but it doesn't matter. You can use any craft for these comparisons, providing it is one that you can visualize easily. Conversion figures for dimensions are given at the end of the book. Imperial sizes continue to be used with boats, so I use them. To help you to understand the appearance of the boat about to come under discussion this is it approaching the shore on a calm day.

DCA References.
Here I am about to quote from a **DCA Bulletin** and give the number of the **issue 109** and the **page 12** where the article describing a Torch dinghy is to be found; written like this **109/12**. Sometimes I may only refer to the bulletin number; looking for the page involves the searcher in reading other very interesting and useful material. 109 is an old publication, but this does not matter. The information is still just as relevant for this kind of boat. Additionally, the fact that you do not have the article before you, does not matter, as what is written here, in this publication, will stand alone without it. It is my intention to give reference numbers in this way for the DCA articles to which I refer. This will allow anyone intent on discovering as

much as they can about any particular aspect of subjects that may interest them, to read wider, to gather more information and to facilitate checking. My references will not include EVERY article available on the subject, but just a sample. In almost every case there will be much more material. The Bulletin contents list is divided into sections for ease of access. As an example, the first section is *'Descriptions of classes or types of boats, comments on cruising performance, choice of boat.'* Going back to the end of 2004 there were over 550 entries covering virtually every kind of craft (See sample at end of book), they have been added to since.

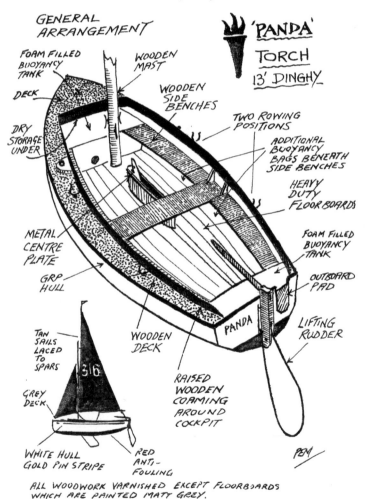

GENERAL ARRANGEMENT

'PANDA' TORCH 13' DINGHY

FOAM FILLED BUOYANCY TANK

WOODEN MAST

WOODEN SIDE BENCHES

DECK

TWO ROWING POSITIONS

DRY STORAGE UNDER

ADDITIONAL BUOYANCY BAGS BENEATH SIDE BENCHES

HEAVY DUTY FLOORBOARDS

METAL CENTRE PLATE

FOAM FILLED BUOYANCY TANK

GRP HULL

OUTBOARD PAD

TAN SAILS LACED TO SPARS

PANDA

LIFTING RUDDER

316

WOODEN DECK

GREY DECK

RAISED WOODEN COAMING AROUND COCKPIT

PEM

WHITE HULL GOLD PIN STRIPE

RED ANTI-FOULING

ALL WOODWORK VARNISHED EXCEPT FLOORBOARDS WHICH ARE PAINTED MATT GREY.

In the Torch article, to which I will now refer there are four very good diagrams with lots of visual detail, (the full page sketch is included here as an illustration of what might be found in DCA articles) and there is a practical write-up giving a bit of history and explaining what the owners feel about their boat. Incidentally, this is not an illustration of my own boat, which is actually called 'Tyne'.

More about Dimensions.
My Torch dinghy was my basic starting point for dimensions. It was designed as a moderate, but safe sailer without any racing aspirations. According to the article these (see below), are its dimensions, BUT all such statistics should only be viewed as 'guidance'. My boat has a wooden centreboard and therefore should be lighter, but when I actually weighed it, totally stripped, it was 25lbs heavier. Let's say they might 'average' 240lbs.

Torch class. (Peter & Averil Merrin's 'Panda' DCA Bull. No. 109/12)
Length 13ft.
Sail Area 80 sq. ft. Weight 228lbs (Metal centreplate)
Beam 5ft 1ins (A rough guide to space and stiffness)

Now that we have the statistics from one craft, the Torch, we can compare them with a similar craft. Whilst there is an illustration for this next boat in the bulletin, it is not essential to be able to see it. The point that is being made here is that you can begin to create an image of how one hull will compare with another, just by looking at a few sizes, so I have no need to reproduce the diagram. It might even be advantageous NOT to be able to see the boat, as this will encourage visualizing its approximate form and accentuate any differences.

Mayfly class. (Liz Baker's, 'Black Swan' DCA Bull. No106/15)
Length 12ft 9ins
Sail area 90 sq. ft. Weight 210 lbs
Beam 5ft 6ins
It will be noticed that this boat whilst having a similar length has more sail area, similar (slightly less) weight, but the major difference is in the beam where the boat is much broader than the Torch and will therefore stand up to its sail for longer and develop more power.
        This particular article has six pages describing the boat, the modifications, learning to cruise and what worked and what didn't.

Once again, although it was written a long time ago every word still remains completely relevant especially to anyone at the beginning of the dinghy cruising learning process. What else might we learn as we look at a few other boats?

Here is another craft the very popular Wanderer class developed from the Wayfarer. This may well be the best craft for most people to use as a 'Yardstick' when making comparisons between boats, as it is much more widely known than the first two classes I have mentioned above.

Wanderer Class. (Margaret Dye 'Wanderbug' DCA Bull. No. 91/13)
Length 14ft
Sail Area 109 sq. ft. Weight 275 lbs
Beam 5ft 10ins
This class of dinghy is the star of Margaret's book on dinghy cruising that I mentioned at the beginning of this book. Her book has many descriptions of its performance under a variety of conditions and several photographs to establish a good all-round image of its capabilities. (See also excess buoyancy 215/15).
How does it compare with the boats we have just mentioned?

One foot in length (compared with the Torch) makes a lot of difference in dinghies of this size, as to some extent, length also equates to speed. The Wanderer carries 29 sq. ft. of sail more than the Torch, whilst its weight (almost surprisingly) is not enormously different, but once again, the beam and therefore the stiffness of the boat will give it a much more powerful performance when the wind begins to blow. In very light winds it is possible that the more slender Torch might hold its own, though lack of sail area might tell against it. The narrowness of the Torch can also be one of its 'secret' advantages when it comes to rowing (see Rowing. Ch. 3).

Roughly similar craft such as these three might now form the core of our understanding about dimensions, so that when more unusual boats comes along (**I do not 'recommend' these, they are simply 'dimensions', as examples.**) it is possible to evaluate them more meaningfully. *Unusual craft 1.*
A rowing/sailing skiff (L. J. Shields 'American Pie' Bull. No. 92/14)
Length 14ft
Sail Area 67 sq ft. Sailing weight 140lbs
Beam 3ft 6ins
Straight away one sees this to be a very lightweight but skinny craft. Equal in length to the Wanderer it is only half its weight (because primarily it is for rowing), but it is so slender that it will be difficult for

the crew to move outwards to counteract sail forces, so sail area needs to be restricted. The instant impression is of an easily driven, light craft, but one that is capable of providing exciting times under sail and may take you swimming unless handled with care.

Another American craft, this time a commercially marketed boat was described by Martin Cooperman (DCA Bull. No. 108/08).
Javelin class. *Unusual craft 2.*
Length 14ft
Sail Area 125 sq. ft. Hull weight 475lbs. Trailing weight 575lbs.
Beam 5ft 8ins
These dimensions start off by being very comparable with the Wanderer, and then suddenly we see the weight, which is almost double. Closer reading of the specification in the original article shows that the centreboard alone weighs 49 lbs so it becomes clear that this craft is beginning to use weight as ballast to generate stability in addition to the shape of the craft. It will probably give a very steady ride, changing speed only gradually as the wind rises and being slow to heel, but it should punch well to windward giving a heavier 'keel boat' feel with its motion in waves.

If we return to the Torch at this point we can see how within similar overall lengths we are now getting a completely different boat when we put it alongside the Javelin, but this is nowhere near the limit of the differences that are possible.

One of the most highly regarded cruising dinghies is the Roamer that was specially designed for the job of cruising by Eric Coleman (the man who started the DCA). It has been described in several DCA bulletins, but several pages in Bulletin No. 100 pull these descriptive dimensions together.

Roamer. 214/16
Length 14ft
Working sail area 96 sq. ft. Weight 760 lbs
Beam 5ft 10ins.
Yes, the weight is three times that of the Wanderer for slightly less sail area. It carries 76lbs of internal ballast and uses a centreboard weighing 80lbs. Clearly it will not be as fast as the Wanderer but as I have already pointed out, speed is not everything in the cruising game. The performance of the Roamer is quite satisfactory for cruising and the stronger the wind blows the more solid it will feel compared to its lighter-weight friends. It has the luxury of fixed berths and accommodation and is self-righting (if it can be ever be persuaded onto its beam ends). A boat such as this will be at home

on salt water and is capable of passage making because it is really a 'pocket cruiser' that looks like a dinghy, having somehow straddled an invisible line that separates it from the lighter, open true dinghy. (Building plans may be purchased from the DCA.)

Having looked at basic dimensions and tried to grasp what they mean it might now be possible to look at your own boat if you have one. How does it compare to the ones that we have discussed here? Is it bigger? Smaller? How wide? What sail area? Then, maybe most important of all, do you think that it might be suitable for the way that you would like use it, as discovered in the answers that you gave to the personal questionnaire?

Building boats.
Maybe you haven't got a boat? If this is the case then you will probably have to consider buying one or there is a remote possibility that you might consider building one. This latter option is probably not to be encouraged unless you have some boatbuilding or allied craft experience. Building boats goes into a whole different sphere. The most popular self-build design is still the Mirror 11 that from the outset was sold as a construction kit. It was said, at one time (untruly), that there were more kits under beds in spare rooms, than there were afloat. This reflected not on the boat, but on the failure of romantic dreamers to appreciate the amount of sheer hard graft that is required to build a boat, even a small one. (See, Kit Building later) It is more cost effective to buy a boat than to build one. This book is about the 'Practical' dinghy cruiser (the person, as well as the qualities of the boat), but it must be recognized that everybody has their own 'practical level' of ability with tools and equipment. Boatbuilding needs a high level of ability and anyone undertaking it should be confident that they will be able to see everything through to a successful conclusion before they even begin. It is good to be encouraged by boat construction articles in magazines. Reading about all aspects of boats and their construction is to be recommended, but having some cruising experience before embarking on the construction of a cruising craft seems to be a self-evident requirement.

Designing and building your own boat is an 'ultimate challenge'. The main motivation would be that you have already gained a great deal of direct experience and superior knowledge, then have evolved new ideas that can only be expressed fully in a new specialist craft. There are examples of this in DCA literature and it is fascinating for experienced sailors to read in-depth articles by Eric Coleman, John Perry and Peter Bick about all aspects of cruising dinghy design. If you just want to learn to cruise, look at existing classes of dinghies (See the end of the book) that offer a wide variety of choice and select the one that is nearest to your criteria. It is much cheaper, considerably quicker and probably a lot safer.

... for something completely different.

I would not want to move on without saying that whilst the core of dinghy cruising people are conventional in that they use fairly sedate craft, usually with a sloop rig, there are also some fascinating exceptions that force anyone to challenge the validity of conventional wisdom. I will select just three craft to illustrate this and it is of interest to compare their sailing weights. I cannot indulge in full descriptions except to say that they demonstrate how many solutions there are to the challenges of dinghy cruising. I have observed that these boats attract attention wherever they go, as they excite curiosity, interest and discussion.

Paradox Class. Boat 'Little Jim.'
(Alastair Law. 181/36, 196/34. Gilchrist /Law 193/45)
Designed by Matt Layden.
Length OA. 13'-10" (4.2m.) Beam 4-0" (1.23m)
Sail area. 9.3 sq. m.
Displacement 640kg (1400 lbs)

Basically a rectangular sectioned hull, topped with a raised, glazed cabin. It is flat bottomed with no board or keel, just shaped chine runners extending horizontally from the bottom corners of the hull. It uses ballast and water ballast. It is sailed completely from inside, using a steering line that circles the cabin. The roughly square sail sets on an unstayed mast and is set and rolled away like a blind, using lines that lead inside. Manual propulsion is by yuloh (like a sculling oar).

Practical Dinghy Cruiser

The Explorer. (Jones / Muscott and Mitchell. 184/17, 185/73, 189/30, 195/39, 196/29,) Designed and built by Mukti Mitchell. Boat test report was published in Practical Boat Owner 459 March 2005.
Displacement 360 kgs (800 lbs)
Sail Area. 10.02 sq. m. (110 sq. ft.)
Draft. Keel up. 1.4 ft (0.43m). Keel Down. 5' (1.52m)
The main innovative development on this boat is its swinging ballasted-bulb keel that allows it to be lowered in deep water and

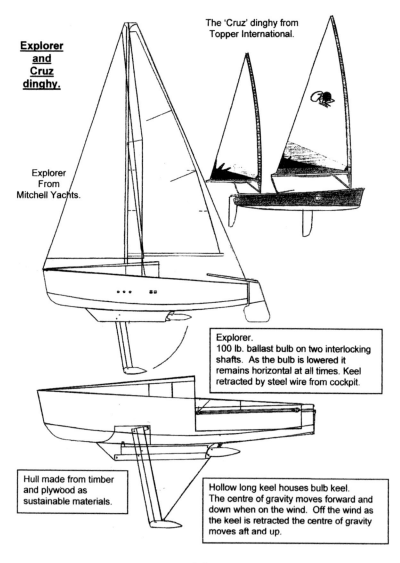

Explorer and Cruz dinghy.

The 'Cruz' dinghy from Topper International.

Explorer From Mitchell Yachts.

Explorer.
100 lb. ballast bulb on two interlocking shafts. As the bulb is lowered it remains horizontal at all times. Keel retracted by steel wire from cockpit.

Hull made from timber and plywood as sustainable materials.

Hollow long keel houses bulb keel. The centre of gravity moves forward and down when on the wind. Off the wind as the keel is retracted the centre of gravity moves aft and up.

then raised to give her a shallow draught in shoal waters. This has clear benefits for performance and self-righting ability. The boat has been used to promote a 'Low Carbon Lifestyle'. The idea is that going away on holiday, locally, in a sailing boat primarily made from renewable materials, is much less harmful to the environment from the viewpoint of carbon emissions than, say, flying to stay in an hotel complex overseas.

Geese.
(John Lidstone.181/46, 185/64) Designed + built John Lidstone.
Length OA 16'–4". Beam 8'–10" Sail A.80sq.ft. Hull weight.140 lbs.
At first glance this looks like a proa, but it does not travel both backwards and forwards as they do. It is more truly a canoe stabilised with an outrigger, which sails in a conventional manner

Geese beached with other DCA boats

having a single sail on a mast that does not use shrouds. This means that the outrigger is positioned on either side according to which tack the boat is on. The boat is beautifully made, and as light as a feather yet very stable. It is possible to dismantle and transport it on a car roof, though a trailer is preferred. It has 'speed capability', but it sails securely even in heavy winds.

27

Dinghy Classes.

Having carefully considered the fundamentals, most people would look closely at the existing dinghy classes where a general choice has to be made. There is no one perfect craft, only a series of compromises and you have to decide on each of them for yourself.

It helps to know what craft are available, so magazines, books and the Internet are starting points. Then there is the local sailing club, but most of the craft to be found there will usually be racing oriented and often the club itself will dictate the main classes. Racing has had a powerful general influence on dinghy design and it will be certain that the current hotshot classes are not going to be suitable for cruising.

It is sometimes more fruitful to seek in the furthest reaches of the dinghy park or boatyard to see what is tucked away in corners. Older, fatter, slower, but solidly constructed and well cared for, at a reasonable price, are some of the qualities that might become attractive in the search.

What dinghies do other people use?

The Dinghy Cruising Association lists its members and their boats, so their boats are therefore already 'in use' as cruisers. They cover just about everything. Some that have cropped up regularly over the years are referred to here with brief comments. DCA references won't be given for all types. These references and this selection of classes are by no means exhaustive, but a longer list is included at the end of the book. There are literally hundreds to choose from and this is mainly British boats. Other countries have their own locally favoured types. As each craft is mentioned there will be lessons to be learned that are generally applicable to other types. No boat will be perfect.

The Mirror dinghy. DCA Bull Nos. (*Vintage*) 76/17 Roger Gomm, 78/13 John Perry, 81/06, John Gray, 101/10, Ted Jones 102/17 (*more modern*) Dave Sumner.161/38, 162/32, 170/32, 174/14, 179/26, 182/37, 184/36. 188/42, 191/33, 196/43. This dinghy has been popular because it is short, lightweight and available for self-build. As it is a wooden boat, owners feel confident making modifications that they might not undertake on a GRP hull. It can be moved on the top of a car. Although only 10ft 10ins long it offers the space of a larger craft because its bow has been 'cut off'; if it was extended to become pointed it might be 12ft long. The main 'weaknesses' that might need modifying for cruising seem to be:

- the thin 6mm foot well floor seems vulnerable to fatigue and damage on rough ground
- the daggerboard fouls the boom when raised
- the standard (sliding) gunter rig has to be modified for deep reefing, (but see David Sumner 208/34)
- to provide sheltered cruising storage the buoyancy tanks will need to be modified. (Cliff Martin 208/37)

However it must be remembered that ALL other dinghies will also have features that could be made better. Many improvements and extra additions will be needed to convert them into a craft suited to cruising. It helps if you have a liking for a bit of DIY, as this is almost inescapable. This is where the 'Practical' element becomes important. Most dinghy cruising people are ready to have-a-go.

GP 14. DCA Bull. No. 75/11 P. Philpott, 130/39, Stocks.
Enterprise see Steve Bradwell 211/43. Gull see Chris Abela 41/215. The large standard rigs provide a racy performance and may need reducing in size.

Wayfarer. This is perhaps the most widely used cruising dinghy class. Much of its early popularity stemmed from the exploits of Frank Dye and the people who sailed with him, both offshore and inland. There is a strong class association that educates and encourages its members in the skills of dinghy cruising. At 16ft it is a big boat and usually requires two people to handle it in comfort, especially in launching and recovering ashore. It might be thought that this boat is the perfect craft for dinghy cruising, but as with all craft it will be found to have limits that could make another craft more suited for an individual's needs.

Mirror 16.
Like the Wayfarer they are big and powerful with the advantage of a flat floor, but they are of wooden construction, they are ageing and only a limited number are available now (see centre pages).

A bit about Wood.
Maybe this is the time to say that wood as a material has some wonderful qualities, especially its stiffness compared to its weight and also its beauty, but it also has some drawbacks that should not be ignored. Its primary function, the very task for which it was designed in nature, is to absorb water and conduct it along inside its structure. In a living tree the wood is always totally waterlogged.

Wood continues sucking in water (and changing shape) even when it's not in the tree. Something else. As the planet has progressed, a whole host of insects and organisms have evolved to live on wood. Various fungi just lick their lips when they find it, especially in dark places. Wood cannot last forever. It hardens and becomes brittle losing the springiness of its youth, just like me. There are old traditionally constructed, wooden boats about, but restoring them is a whole specialist ball-game requiring knowledge and skills beyond the beginner. Take my advice and avoid elderly, traditionally built, clinker dinghies that have solid wooden planks and metal fastenings, no matter how beautiful they look gleaming away in the June sunshine. Glued clinker, ply panels and epoxy sheathing are a different matter, but even here the age of thin plywood (that could be losing its durability), is something that should be carefully weighed in the balance. Wooden structures in water are probably only as good as the plastic between the pieces (glues and mastics) and the integrity of their plastic coatings (paints) that have to protect the timber from water contact. As someone who has studied wood, worked with wood and even taught wood, I prefer the outside of my hull to have a nice thick plastic coating, one which is usually described as fiberglass or epoxy sheathing. Wood is much better used elsewhere. There are many good wooden boats about, but just be aware that if you choose wood you are also choosing to do all the maintenance work that goes with wood. It is never ending. Finally, for the beginner, do not listen to anybody who says a wooden boat is only 'taking up'. They are talking about it leaking.

Drascombe Lugger.
This appears to be the most popular of the Drascombe range of cruising craft (designed by John Watkinson and named after his Devon farmhouse). The Drascombes whilst being essentially open boats are heavy enough to behave like and almost be classed as, small cruisers. Their rugged construction and low sailplan make them good cruisers. They tend to use outboards rather than oars.

Rebell. (DCA Bull 46 &106) An Eric Coleman design.
Length 17ft 1ins. Beam 6ft 3ins.
Working Sail Area 119sq ft. Trail Weight 1000lbs (Ballast 160lbs)
It has similar dimensions to the Wayfarer with fixed accommodation, but looks like a big open dinghy with a cuddy. It is a 'pocket cruiser'. (Construction plans available from the DCA.)

Where are the new boats?
So far, the boats that I have highlighted have been what might be called 'older' designs. The reason for this is that they have established themselves over the years and their performance is understood. The companies that constructed them may have come and gone or been replaced by others. So why haven't I been comparing newer boats? In part, this is because I cannot guarantee the current status of their production runs, the solvency of their builders and whether some even newer design is about to corner the market, due to its perfection in fulfilling the cruising brief. Or maybe it is going to disappear without trace, because of its unsuitability for purpose? I cannot heap cruising praise upon, nor condemn boats that I have not dinghy cruised. Sailing a boat is not the same as dinghy cruising it, so you always tend to be an outside observer watching 'other-people-cruising-other-craft' and not really experiencing the boats for yourself. You learn about different boat's qualities by this external observation over a period of time and by the reports of others. (In a moment I shall try to illustrate my meaning by using the story of the Cruz.) Very few sailors will have had more than three / five cruising dinghies in their lives and the time span of their ownership will extend so far back that their early craft will now be 'older' designs. Anyone interested in the newer craft available must recognise that they will be in a different price bracket, one that is related to the commercial values of today, but the advantage of this is that they should retain their second hand value when it comes to resale. Depending on their newness they should be structurally sound and virtually free from all kinds of decay and deterioration, thus saving much work.

To seek a new boat you must study the latest magazines and read the reports, look at the pictures and go to the boat shows as well as trawling the Internet. As I write this I can say that it will be difficult to find a brand new, totally kitted-out, dinghy cruising boat for sale. I have recently seen some that come quite close (see appendix), but the challenge of all the different kinds of cruising means that no commercial builder has yet successfully managed to cover every demand in a single, stock craft. There are just too many variables that must be resolved to be able to specify everything that the final product should include, exactly, for you, within its design. You must look and see for yourself. All craft will need customizing, even good ones like the Laser 16. One commercial manufacturer that ventured into this 'niche' field was Topper International in the early 1990's who produced a craft called the 'Cruz'. (Back Cover)

<u>Topper Cruz. (See earlier diagram, page 26.)</u>
Length O. A. 14'- 4". Beam 5'- 11"
Working sail area. 113 sq.ft. Weight 265 lbs.

When first produced it was an unusual concept, in that it was a ketch, setting its sails by sleeving them onto unstayed masts. It was quite well received and continues to be used, but it has not become the runaway success that one might have hoped for, in a product designed specifically for a specialist market. It is interesting to see how articles about it have progressed in the DCA bulletin. A comprehensive description of a test sail by Peter Bick was published in 1995 (147/24) to be followed by owners experiences of it after sailing, in 1998/9 (G. Saffrey. 161/45, B. Jones 162/16). In these accounts they speak of their impressions and outline some of the modifications and equipment that they found necessary in order to dinghy cruise the craft. In 1999 (165/46) a straightforward cruise account 'Sail the Savage Solway' by Colin Firth describes a weekend sail with two Cruz dinghies sailing together. He includes a number of observations about the boats qualities in different conditions, but the emphasis of the article had now shifted from simply reporting on the boat, towards describing the events of the voyage itself. One idiosyncrasy of the boat is the mizzen mast position forward of the tiller. This potentially, to some extent, restricts the movement of the tiller and its extension. Peter Bick mentioned this point in the very beginning. The tiller must either be short, or be 'looped' or 'Y' shaped, to operate around the mast. In 2005 (10 years after the first report), Mike Jackson won the DCA's Peter Bick Technical Trophy by describing a tiller modification to operate the rudder around the mast using a control-wire linkage. To come even more up to date, there is now a Topper Cruz Forum for exchanging ideas on the Internet, so things are still developing.

I hope this illustrates how tricky it would be to make immediate judgments about a craft that has newly arrived on the market. It takes some time before a true picture emerges and for its qualities to be stated reliably. Having said this, there are 'new' boats out there and each person must research them to their own satisfaction. It is worth mentioning that the latest generation of boats has taken advantage of Computer Aided Design. This has allowed them to evolve the use of water ballast and included self-righting qualities. Their component parts can be planned and produced by computer guided cutting machines to save a great deal of time in construction (199/43) so there are still significant advances being made and you should research them. The Internet has made this process a great deal swifter and easier. As a starting point access any 'Small Sailboats' site (see end of book) for this and other suggestions.

The time has come ...
In the design of almost any object there seems to come a moment for similar solutions to evolve, as several people are exploring the same concepts at the same time, often widely separated from each other. I think that I perceive an evolving trend towards the 'deep' dinghy-cruising craft, because a design concept is arriving from various different directions. I will give a brief outline so that you can understand my meaning and perhaps take up the story yourself.

Deep Dinghy – the chronology.
(I will include website addresses where they are available, not including the www. or the http.) The codes give the 'Dinghy Cruiser' bulletin numbers; **note** how they are almost continuous.
The underlines emphasise some of the evolving common features.
208/08 From New Zealand, John Welsford, Well known for designs such as 18'-2" blue water voyager, 'Swaggie' (jwboatdesigns.co.nz) mentioned in a letter that he had been commissioned to design a boat called SCAMP.
208/69 A joint article by Josh Colvin, & Craig Wagner the editors of Small Craft Advisor (smallcraftadvisor.com) and John Welsford gave outline details of the projected cruising dinghy SCAMP, only 10'- 4" in length that was based on one of John's earlier designs, the 'Sherpa' tender.
209/32 An article by Dr. Chris Waite explained how some time previously he had evolved a 15'-6" (mainhull), plywood craft called 'Tit Willow' (see centre pages} that had initially been intended as a half-scale prototype for a larger steel craft. He had constructed the craft in Muscat, Oman and eventually brought the boat back to England. Although very heavy (it carried 770lbs of ballast) it had a distinctive hull form using a high tumblehome strake above a very curving sheer line. This produced a deep craft with a protected cockpit. The interior bow bulkhead and boxed seating design in the cockpit with a forward cuddy looked very interesting. He described her as 'a small yacht, not a large dinghy.'
210/56 John Welsford's article 'The evolution of SCAMP' explained how he had worked up the design with Josh Colvin and Kees Prins resulting in a modification of dimensions, which now became Length 11'-11", Beam 5'- 4", Water Ballast 173lbs, Approx weight 420 lbs. Paul Lohr wrote about constructing a rudder blade for the

boat. It had a <u>flat bottom</u> and a <u>high freeboard</u> together with a distinctive bow-transom to <u>maximise internal space</u> in relation to overall length.

211/55 a comprehensive **S**mall **C**raft **A**dvisor (**M**arine **P**roject) article 'SCAMP Evaluation' by Howard Rice told the story of a short proving cruise and showed pictures of the boat.

211/39 'Just what is a Cruising Dinghy?' by John Welsford had a number of photographs of his designs. His 17ft Pathfinder design had several features showing affinity with Chris Waite's 'Tit Willow' and the transom shots of both boats appeared similar in form. His 16'-5" Pilgrim design was described as '<u>full bodied</u> with <u>wide side decks</u> and high coamings'. The cockpit boxed seating/buoyancy towards the stern appeared in both boats.

Issue 95/31 of **Water Craft** magazine (watercraftmagazine.com) carried a picture of Chris Waite's latest evolution of his design thinking called the 'Premise 12' (see our centre pages). It was described as a sail-and-oar dinghy blending features of the Grand Banks dory with the Thames Barge (flat bottom). It used a high <u>internally-bulkheaded bow</u> conventionally shaped, <u>deep topsides</u> and <u>water ballast</u>. It is <u>11'- 6" long</u> with a <u>cuddy</u> and '<u>flotation before swamping' side decks</u>.

216/10 A letter from Chris Waite explains his thinking, mentions a previous 60 mile rowing/cruising trial undertaken on the River Thames. He makes useful observations about filling and draining its <u>water ballast</u> tanks. (See, 'Polly Wee' centre pages)

It is quite clear from further reading, that the craft forms mentioned here have been independently evolved. They are producing a new form of dinghy-cruising craft by arriving at similar solutions. The internal depth of these boats offers greatly enhanced protection to the cockpit area. The use of water ballast, long championed by Swallow Boats (<u>swallowboats.com</u>), amongst others, allows a reduction in drag when rowing or seeking performance (tanks empty), but stability when sailing (tanks full). Here we can see the water ballast arrangement below the cockpit sole in 'Polly Wee', Chris Waite's deep dinghy.

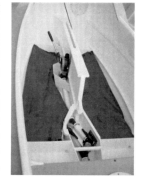

This is an ongoing story. Small Craft Advisor are offering plans and kits and for anyone seriously interested in the SCAMP and this looks like a potential route to follow. BUT. You must evaluate the ideas yourself. A high bow might offer protection, but how will the boat lie to wind when stopped? What do you think about the transom-bow for the use that you have in mind? Will the rig suit your circumstances or do you prefer an alternative? If so, why? What is the capacity of a totally swamped cockpit? Could the water be removed? How? (Enter 'Polly Wee takes a bath.' on YouTube, by portnastorm) to see capsize testing of the empty boat. If you managed to achieve an inverted capsize how would the boat behave? It is decision time again. You really need to know and understand about every aspect of these things and ask the right questions.

I have written nothing about water ballast but it is a fascinating subject filled with experimental potential. How much, Where? How do you fill it? How do you empty it? All this is at the cutting edge of design thinking and it is probably not for the beginner, but it is interesting to observe the efforts of the brave people who invest so much time, money and expertise in pushing the boundaries outwards.

Kit building.
Mention of kit building prompts a look at the latest methods. This is a big topic and I can only swiftly skim it here to open up the subject for your further investigation. The KL canoe and then the humble Mirror dinghy demonstrated a building method of attaching plywood panels to each other as well as protecting them by using modern resins and cloths. This technique has been expanded and refined over the years.

Polly Wee Torture Ply Hull

Today the boat form and the plywood panels are designed on computers (**CAD C**omputer **A**ided **D**esign) and the panels are then accurately set out and commercially cut out, usually using (**CNC C**omputer **N**umerate **C**ontrol) router machines. The shapes are left with a little final cutting to be done, so that the panels remain attached to their plywood sheets ready to be released by joining the cuts. Panels can then be precisely bevelled and locating tabs and slots can assist in the accurate alignment of the components.

Investigate: fyneboatkits.co.uk, or jordanboats.co.uk. This latter company will guide you towards construction videos or contacts in other countries.

Craft types and actually 'living' in a small boat.

So far this has all been about the boat, but the second major element to consider is the whole process of living aboard. For most newcomers it is this aspect that contains the most 'mystery'. What is it like to sleep on such a craft? What do you do? A number of aspects are very honestly covered by Cliff Martin (see centre pages) in 'Comfort on a dinghy cruise.' 195/32. The boat that he refers to is the 'quite small' Mirror dinghy. Like him, I would begin by not painting too rosy a picture. We are in the area of realism not romanticism. It's a bit like camping, but when you are camping you have more space, because you routinely go outside and walk about doing different things. On a boat, you don't, unless you 'park' ashore, but even then, it is not a simple story. Let's go back to camping. Camping is a good starting point, but I'm not going to make it sound easy. First I'll remind you about the basic boat types.

There are some fundamental differences between living in an open dinghy and in the lidded dinghy or 'pocket cruiser' that I have already described. The practical differences are mainly concerned with the onboard organization of equipment and also personal management.

Internal organisation and management.

In an open dinghy all the domestic living systems are packed away during sailing time. The pans, the galley, the deflated mattress, the compressed sleeping bag etc. are carefully stored so that they do not interfere with the sailing systems, but also to keep them, as much as possible, from contact with water which might be splashed aboard. This is not the case on a 'pocket cruiser'. Almost all of the domestic equipment can remain loosely secured in its functional place below deck. This difference radically changes the way the boats are usually used.

On a craft with a small cabin the crew can pop below to put on the kettle, or snatch a quick lie down on a bunk whilst not on duty. All the gear is open and exposed within the cabin that protects it. It means that the chance of a potential capsize must be reduced to an absolute minimum. This usually means having ballast aboard. It should always go without saying that (unballasted) open-dinghy sailors **do not intend to capsize**, but they must always recognise the vague, but real possibility, no matter how unlikely it may be, so they secure their gear and sail their boats accordingly.

For monohull craft, ensuring that they will not capsize by using ballast, instantly leads to a leap in the all-up weight of the boat. Putting a hard cuddy or cabin onto an open dinghy almost inevitably requires the addition of ballast to ensure stability, thus changing the character of the craft, both in sailing and in recovery and trailing modes. In the constant search for the perfect cruising dinghy designers face some conflicting requirements, as most people want the security of the pocket cruiser, together with the lightness and mobility of the open dinghy. These qualities are hard to find together, because there is not really a smooth transition from one craft type to the other. Most craft have to be either an unballasted dinghy without fixed accommodation or to have a lid and ballast and become a 'pocket cruiser'. The division between the types is fairly clear.

Organisation. What it really means.
Whatever the type of small craft used, personal organisation is very important. The smaller the boat, the better organised its crew must be. You could experience this at home, by erecting a very small (two man) tent in the garden. Put inside it the galley equipment with food, a change of clothes and the sleeping gear. Put on your oilskins, boots, lifejacket etc. thoroughly wet them then squeeze into the tent. You are no longer allowed to step outside.

The simple process of taking off the oilies, boots and lifejacket, changing clothes then cooking and eating a meal, followed by making up the bed and getting into it, within the restrictions of the tent will instantly illustrate how one must have 'ways of doing things' when operating within such a confined space. Wet oilies/lifejackets/boots cannot just be discarded anywhere, they have to be folded and packed tightly to occupy as little internal space as possible, then placed, probably somewhere near to the entrance so as to restrict the spread of water throughout the accommodation.

Lack of headroom, the flatness of the floor, the mental forward planning required for each simple task, all conspire to make the exercise very tiring. Add to this the constant movement of a small boat afloat and scatter the base of the tent with a pair of oars, sundry lengths of rope, ground tackle, bucket, bailer and spare sails etc. and you will begin to appreciate how each move must be planned with care if the whole interior is not just to become a total clutter of unmanageable kit slowly sliding down into a wet bilge. The ultimate problem would be to add another person into this tiny space, also clad in wet sailing gear with an enormous bin bag full of their bedding and change of clothes. Then would come the problem that is never mentioned. In this same space, use the toilet whilst your friend is preparing a meal or doing the washing up.

The open dinghy approximates fairly closely to this experiment with the tent. There is a fundamental, key issue to be appreciated here. The tent (and the open boat) does not offer, nor impose, any organisation. In the open dinghy the domestic gear must be cleared away each day to leave the area stripped clear for the functions of sailing. A lidded dinghy, however, will have fixed positions for bunks and the galley at least. It separates the two basic functional areas. Sailing is **outside** in the cockpit. Domestic arrangements are **inside**. This, (amongst other things) should offer the chance, for example, of agreeing a system for use of the toilet, if that should be necessary. The result is that the 'pocket cruiser' offers a built-in degree of organisation that is permanently visible (storage shelves, clothes hooks etc,) to assist in the continuous management of all aspects of sailing and living, by basically keeping the domestic functions (below deck), separate from the sailing functions (on deck). The open dinghy doesn't do this.

The time it takes to convert a small, open sailing dinghy into living accommodation with a degree of comfort should not be underestimated. To secure the boat, pack away the sailing systems, erect the tent, change clothes, assemble the galley and the bed then get something to eat, would probably take a beginner about two hours (in good weather) depending on their systems. To do the same in a pocket cruiser it would be nearer to half an hour and could be compressed further if necessary. Two hours of work at the beginning and at the end of each sailing day (when the crew can be exhausted) is too much work. There is a strong incentive to either, simplify and speed up the process, or use a dinghy with a lid. How will you feel? Are you really, really sure that you can be, or want to be, a dinghy cruiser?

Some reasons for my dinghy cruising.
I hope that this has made you think about the practical realities. I also hope that it has not made you discard the whole project. There is more to dinghy cruising than discomfort. Perhaps we might return to myself and look at some of the circumstances that have given me enjoyment in dinghy cruising. And in addition, let's also include

something which has, so far, been set aside. Having looked and listed, read and explored, pondered at length about what the boat will be used for and where it will go, you finally make a choice of craft, or take another look at the craft that you already have. One factor not yet discussed may well turn out to be the most important one of all. How much money is available?

Finance, Fabrication and Philosophy.
Going to buy a new Wayfarer with a trailer currently costs about 50 times what I paid for my unfashionable, second hand, ex-sailing-centre dinghy. Buying a self-righting, purpose designed, bespoke built specialist craft will cost several times more. The boats are not the same of course, but my boat suits my choice of sailing activity perfectly. The bigger boats (being heavier) would not fulfill my requirements as well as my smaller, lighter craft.

Sailing on a shoestring is one of my more important requirements, not necessarily because I am financially challenged (poor!). I find that it is within my nature to invent and innovate. I like making things and I feel especially rewarded if I can construct something from simple materials which will function just as well as an expensive alternative. I respond to the challenges of sailing, but I enjoy analysing the problems that I find and trying to make devices to improve my efficiency, or increase my comfort, within the natural boundaries of the activity that I have chosen to follow. It would not be as much fun for me to buy an expensive craft with all the cruising systems in place (even if that was possible), as it would be to acquire an old boat and methodically invent and fabricate what I found I needed. This is my personal requirement because I am a practical, self-sufficient person, but it may not be for other people.

There are other related considerations, one of which may be thought to be slightly unusual, namely the philosophical and aesthetic experience of sailing. Amongst dinghy cruisers there is a group that subscribe to the notion of 'The smaller the boat, the better the sport.' and additionally 'One person, one boat.' I will attempt to give a small insight into these feelings.

The Dinghy Cruiser.
Cruising can be a solitary pursuit. One person, one boat, somehow sums up how the person concerned has no 'thought distractions' whilst sailing alone and so can concentrate with a clear mind on a single 'waking-dream'. The 'dream' is that internal monologue, a narrative inside the head that interprets the reality of what is

happening and what must be done to respond to the world around. Whilst these feelings can be experienced on a larger craft, the smaller the boat, the more personal it becomes. It is a **personal** experience rather like a rider on a horse or a youth on a motorbike, but with a small boat the bond can be even stronger. The boat isn't just a means of transport; it is the sailor's safety and protection. Maybe it's more like the climber or the diver with their equipment. The boat becomes a life support system.

Then there is the added dimension of increased awareness. The solitary dinghy cruiser enjoys aesthetic experiences, the beauty of the sunsets, wind on the face, motion of the water, strength of the tide and the power of nature conveyed through the craft. The sailor can be frightened, can be forced to endure hardship, but there will never be loneliness, because in the subconscious mind of the sailor the boat shares the experiences and plays its part as the carrier of all that is needed to face the challenge of the hostile environment.

Dinghy cruising, for many who follow it, is not caravanning and it isn't just camping. It is more of an expedition to explore nature, solitude and self-sufficiency. It is physical and mental but also teamwork between the sailor and the boat. Some sailors writing of their experiences refer to themselves as 'We' instead of 'I'. One person, one boat, self-sufficient and with a clear mind, is what it is all about for many dinghy cruisers.

Of course one does not have to feel this way to cruise in a dinghy, but it is worth knowing that there are people who do and it is their firm choice for them to use their type of craft, sailing in their kind of way. Often they can afford and are able to sail, larger more comfortable cruisers, but they choose not to, because that is a different kind of sailing. Not all choices are totally logical. Quirky personal reasons are allowed. Not following the crowd is encouraged, but with the understanding that the further you diverge from the middle ground, the more responsibility you must accept for your choices. Families do cruise (see centre pages and inside rear cover) and children love the 'Swallows and Amazons' life on sheltered water with beaches at hand.

Having set the scene, it is perhaps useful to look at one person's experiences (mine) in converting an old dinghy into a cruising craft. I did it to respond to the problems of inventing and fabricating all the bits. It was a design challenge. I did it because it was not a great drain on my finances. I did it because there is no commercial product on the market that could be bought 'off the shelf' to do what I wanted to do. I did it for adventurous and philosophical reasons and I did it because I happened to have an old boat. Or did I? I should have had a boat, but unfortunately I had managed to lose it. Now that was carelessness wasn't it, or was it laziness?

I have already described my dinghy, which I had owned for quite some time and casually sailed before I had the idea to use it for cruising. As a break from all this intense 'analysis' here is a short story that explains the strange events that became the catalyst, for me, for the idea of cruising. As this and other little stories unfold, they may touch upon some of the issues already mentioned and reinforce their importance in understanding the concept of cruising and the cruising dinghy.

Lost and Found.

I had a dinghy. It was a Torch. Not a 'flashlight' sort of torch, more like an 'Olympic flame' kind of torch; an ice cream cone with a flame coming out of the top. That image was once the symbol used on road signs to indicate a school and the burning flame of learning.

The dinghy had been designed specifically to teach people to sail in it and it carried the sign of the flaming cornet on its sail to announce itself. Its hull was deep so that you sat in it, rather than on it. It was simple and basic with everything tied together and hardly a shackle anywhere, lanyards instead of rigging screws and a crutch where a gooseneck might have been. It was sliding-gunter rigged, with sails lashed onto the spars and it looked a bit like a slow and dumpy GP14.

Years ago it had served its time at educational sailing centres where one of the learners who had benefited from its presence there, had been me. Later I had progressed to being one of the sailing instructors who had used it with beginners and even later still, I was to purchase it when it had come to the end of its useful days, as centres changed to speedier, roomier Wayfarers.

The fleet of old Torches was going cheap to good homes. Did I want one? I had a soft spot for this particular one mainly because I'd always managed to get it to go faster when competing with other similar boats. (I have to confess here that this was a result of tying the main halyard lower down the gaff, thus lifting my sail up that little bit higher and getting a bit more drive from the breeze above the trees.) I chose my bargain, Torch 269 'Tyne' (they had all been named after sea areas) and took the little old lady home on a borrowed trailer.

41

We pottered about on the river for several seasons when the family was young. My boys had quite a good time in her though they never quite took to sailing in a big way. I was busy myself building a bigger boat in the back garden and eventually we spent most of our sailing time on it. The dinghy was mothballed in different places here and there, it was a bit of a liability, but somehow I never quite got around to getting rid of it.

Yet more water flowed under the bridge of life, and I had another sailing project under construction in a hired barn at a farm some miles from home. There was spare space and I moved the dinghy into a corner of the barn for somewhere cheap to put it. Most of its gear went with it. My construction project completed, I half tidied up the barn, but never quite finished the clearance. Force of circumstances now swirls around the story.

My work changed and took me to another part of the country. The farmer who owned the barn retired and sold his farm. My family had grown and flown. Years and years passed and only very occasionally did I sometimes recall that I had once owned a dinghy, which I'd left in the dark corner of a barn many miles away.

The wheel turned full circle. Three employments later I had moved back to the old county and my route to work took me right past the very farm where I had left the little boat. It was no longer farmed. At first I was too busy to take much notice of it, but gradually my curiosity began to grow. I had no right to expect that the boat was still about, but I wondered what its life story had been since I had abandoned it, so negligently. Morning and evening as I drove past, I found myself rehearsing my speech to the farm's new owner when I knocked on his door. It was tricky trying to explain how I came to 'lose' a boat in his barn.

Eventually I could stand it no longer. I stopped my car on the roadside one late autumn evening and walked up the drive. Everything was quiet. I went around the back to have a quick look at the barn and to my amazement it had been converted into a house. A brick wall had been constructed to separate its land from that of the farm. It was now accessed from a different direction. Another wall, of glass, had replaced the old boarded barn doors. There was no chance of my dinghy still being there.

I returned to the farmhouse and knocked on the door. A girl in her late teens answered. I delivered my long-rehearsed speech about leaving my boat years ago and she listened without any sign of recognition. She said, "He's not here at the moment, can you call back again about this time tomorrow? I'll tell him you came." I agreed and walked away in a whirl of wondering.

I'd committed myself now so at least I was going to discover something. The boat must still exist somewhere because whilst it had a wooden deck that could have rotted, it had a glass hull, which couldn't. If they'd burned it then that was my fault, I couldn't blame them. The rent I owed them for keeping the boat there meant that it was probably theirs anyway.

The next day I walked up the drive with butterflies in my tummy. This was it. At last I'd know the truth. I knocked. He answered the door. "Yes?" he said in a flat monotone. I thought he'd know why I was there, but he didn't appear to. I gave him the speech again. I gave it friendly, jolly, with a touch of an apology. He showed no emotion, he was totally neutral. He stepped out of the door and closed it behind him, "Can't say I know anything about a boat?" he said. I immediately felt that he was being defensive. No. I'm being too kind. I knew he was lying. I tried to reassure him. My purpose was not to pursue anyone I simply wanted to know what had happened to it as I had a sentimental curiosity about it. No, he didn't know. There had been lots of people on the site when the barn had been converted, builders, brickies, and tradesmen. I saw what he was implying, but it needed a lorry and a gang of men to move it. Perhaps he could tell me the name of the builders? Difficult ... it had been a long time ago. I was pleasantly insistent. He said he'd look it up in his paperwork, could I leave it a week or so? I agreed.

This time I walked down the drive with my mind in turmoil. I knew he wasn't being straight with me and I didn't know why. I'd absolved him from any responsibility. I only wanted information. What was it that he couldn't tell me? For a whole week I made my journeys arguing the possibilities in my mind, but I couldn't find a solution. Then I was back on his doorstep.

"Yes?" He looked at me blankly. He didn't remember who I was. I told him that I'd been here last week. He'd not done anything. We started again, but he was covering the same ground. We came to the point where he was going to check his paperwork, so I thought I'd try a new angle. I explained I still had the jib and the tiller in the sail bag in my garage and whoever had the boat might be grateful for them. We talked about equipment and I mentioned other things that had been left, did he know where they went? No, anything and everything that had been removed from the barn had *then been stored in an open-sided shed for a while, but it was no longer there. Could I have a look, just to satisfy myself? Reluctantly he agreed, just to get rid of me. We went to the big open shed and poked about amongst odds and ends and it looked like the trail had ended ... except ... behind some old corrugated roofing sheets leaning against the back wall, I spotted a familiar shape protruding. The rounded tip of a piece of wood with rope attached. It was the mast and the gaff with the mainsail still bent on which we extracted from beneath a decade of dust and I was overjoyed. This was the proof I needed and he had to concede, where previously his stance had been that there was nothing to confirm my story. He needed time to make enquiries. Could I come back in a week? Could I? Nothing would keep me away.*

I was now in a different frame of mind. I was going to see this through. The mystery had to be solved. I strode up the drive in a determined manner next time. The girl answered the door. "He's gone away for a week or two." "When will he be back?" She didn't know, but it would be best to leave it for at least three weeks, maybe a month. Whilst I agreed and went away I resolved to keep a watching brief on passing the place each day. This cloak and dagger stuff certainly added spice to the routine of my journey.

At last I spotted that his car was in the drive so I did not hesitate. I knocked on his door. "Yes?" that same flat emotionless response. I told him that he had been getting some information for me and then I waited for his excuse. It didn't come. "Oh yes, I think I might have something for you", he said, "but it'll cost you some money."

"How much?"

"A hundred pounds ... in notes." he added. I thought for a moment. "Do I get the boat?"

"Have you got a trailer?"

"I can get one, but I need a couple of days."

"Come here at eight o'clock, next Friday with the trailer and the money." There was a strong implication of 'No questions asked.' I had to make a quick decision. This was it. I agreed. "Okay."

This was amazing stuff, more like crossing the Iron Curtain than getting a dinghy back, but now I felt certain that I was moving towards some kind of conclusion. I got the money and put it in the requisite plain brown envelope. I borrowed a trailer and got my eldest son to bring his car that had a tow bar.

The night was black as pitch and a thick, icy, driving drizzle instantly soaked everything. My son and I were the only people about. We drove to the farm and turned in the drive, ready to leave.

As soon as I knocked, the door opened. He had his coat on. "Have you got the money?"

"Yes, here it is." He opened the flap and flicked through the notes then pushed them into his pocket. "Follow me." he said and moved swiftly towards his car. I had to run back to our car, as he'd set off down the drive without waiting. I could just see his lights going left out of the entrance as we set off. Towing a trailer we wouldn't catch him if he put his foot down. We turned left and could only distantly make out red tail lights through the whirring windscreen wipers. "We'll never keep up." said my son. Then I saw he was indicating to turn right. He'd only travelled five or six hundred metres and gone into the drive of the neighbouring farm, which was an old manor house. We turned in and followed the drive as it curved around the back passing the house, until it broadened with lawns on either side. His car was stationary, waiting with the engine running. I got out and walked across in the rain. As I came alongside the driver's door he wound down the window a little, turned on his headlights and said, "It's there." At the limit of the beam across the wet grass were the raised shapes of reeds and rushes marking the edge of a naturally landscaped pond in the manor house gardens. Reflecting white amongst the reeds was the low tip of the bow of a semi-submerged boat. He reversed, rotating his car and then with a skidding on the shingle drive, he accelerated away.

My son brought our car closer to discover what was happening and I crossed the grass along the headlamp beam to see what I could find. The boat was filled with the green stagnant water of the pond to the level of her thwart. Her floorboards floated loosely on the water surface. The decks and floorboards looked like rough tree bark where all her varnish and paint had peeled, curled and then been coated in lichen. She had an all-over covering of slimy green algae, betraying the fact that she had probably been in the water for some years.

It took some hours of toiling to empty her, remove her rudder from the transom and drag her from the pond onto the trailer. We were saturated, dirty and grim-faced on the drive homewards, but I was relieved to get her back.

A dinghy is surely just a collection of bits of wood and metal, fibreglass and string isn't it? Why then did I feel that I had rescued my child from a kidnapper's grasp? Can anyone be cruel to a boat?

Upon reflection the answer may be found in the actions of the man who had her. He knew of her whereabouts; he could almost see her from his front door in his neighbour's pond, yet he did not want to admit her condition to me. The secret he attempted to hide from me was maybe akin to that of keeping an animal in conditions of ill treatment. When it became clear that I wasn't going to go away, he probably decided that he would let me see what had happened to the boat, if he could be paid for the revelation. I don't

think I paid for the boat, nor did I pay for the information. The way he revealed the boat's location on that final night showed me that he was getting paid for the discomfort he would feel when I knew the truth. He was being paid for his admission.

I must take my share of the blame. I had been too busy with other things to be concerned about the boat. I somehow thought that no matter where she was, someone would at least be enjoying the use of her, doing what she was designed to do, but now I saw that this was not so.

In my mind she was linked with sunny days and sandy beaches, young children splashing in the water and the lively response as she heeled to the gusts of wind and came alive. It was inconceivable to me that she could be half submerged and left to rot in stinking water simply because that was all she was seen to be worth. Maybe I paid up without a murmur, to ease my guilty conscience about my neglect?

Whatever the truth I felt differently about the boat once I had found her again. I thought that I should carry through a scheme that I had held in my mind since I originally bought her. I would try to find a way to make her suitable for cruising and camping. Together we could have some more good times in the future.

This last sentence might leave you with a nice, cozy feeling. You too might be looking forward to the same kind of good times. Perfect gentle sailing in sunshine, on flat water through a rural scene might be passing through your mind. And so it may be. It does happen and is most enjoyable, so I'm sorry to have to remind you that it may not be all plain sailing. This book is about the wider experiences of dinghy cruising, both good and slightly less comfortable. Remember the practical realities of living in the small tent, that was designed to help you to understand how it can feel to live in a small dinghy. It was a check on whether you can imagine what you could possibly be involving yourself in. I don't want you to feel that you have been misled. If you still want to hear more, I will shortly explain some of the processes involved in converting the boat, but before that, let me recommend that you read another person's dinghy selection, equipping and sailing experiences.

Roger Barnes has long been the President of the DCA and his observations on dinghy cruising have been published regularly in commercial sailing publications. An award winning account in several sections 198/21,199/25, 200/35, 202/34 with pictures and sketches comprehensively discusses the qualities required of a small, open, traditionally constructed dinghy used for open water cruising. The last section tells the story of how he graduated upwards into a larger offshore cruising dinghy by French designer Francois Vivier. A further highly recommended account of his sailing 'On the Edge of The Wild.' is to be found in 214/54.

3.
Working on the boat.

DCA Quotes.

'the aim of the cruise is detail not distance.'

John Gray.

3.
Working on the boat.

Restoration.
Following the losing and finding of my boat I had a craft in about as bad a condition as it was possible to have. I set to work. After I had dried it out and had removed most of the flaking paint and varnish I began to take account of what I had got in the basic structure.

Initially I was happy just to restore it and return it to its sailing condition. This meant checking the state of repair of everything whilst re-varnishing and painting the wooden areas. I was lucky because I had very little rot and the high quality of the original wooden materials in deck, floorboards, seats, centreboard, rudder, tiller, etc. meant that in the main they could be rejuvenated. Being buried in the shed had protected the mast, gaff, and boom along with the running rigging but the sails were brittle with age and in need of replacement. They were the most major financial outlay.

The general approach.
The work that I did, might equate to you finding an old, neglected boat and having to bring it into reasonable sailing condition. The way to do this is to take each component and check every aspect of its construction. This will not be a quick process. It is wood that makes the most work. Inexperienced sailors often make the mistake at this point of stripping and dismantling EVERYTHING and then finding themselves overwhelmed with the enormousness of the task they face. Here's a word of warning about this approach.

Shipwreck.
I would rarely recommend to anybody that they should totally strip down a boat to its smallest pieces all at one time. I have seen this mistake committed quite frequently, especially by new owners who have just acquired a secondhand craft. Total dismantling of everything, should only be done by very experienced people who are confident in their ability to undertake all the many processes required and who have the enduring patience and single-minded drive needed to put it all back together again. If you buy an old boat in sailing condition, choose carefully what to refurbish first. It may be just the outside of the hull. Get it back together if you can, repainted and with all the fittings checked and secured before you take the inside apart. You can do the interior in a gradual way, just the back half, or just the front half, just the rudder or just the

centreboard and only then would you turn to the spars or the sails etc. Ordinary people should set themselves achievable little projects and enjoy using the boat in between, if that is possible,. This step-by-step approach is so important that I will repeat it when I look at 'Maintenance', which is a process akin to this initial refurbishment

I was lucky in the simplicity of my boat's construction and there came a happy day when the boat was re-launched and sailed around to test its systems. It worked, just as before, so this allowed me to turn my mind towards how it might be modified for cruising. Any boat is a series of small systems, and what follows is an outline of what I had in the basic craft and how I subsequently modified it to make the boat into a cruising unit. As I describe the process of my restoration it might be helpful to add selected, occasional relevant background information that has been made available in Dinghy Cruising Association bulletins. This is the point where we have to ease into the practicalities of actually doing some work.

Before going onto the practical processes I should say that I am not intending to offer lessons in glassfibre work, drilling holes for screws, sharpening planes, cleaning paint brushes or any of the other tasks involved. If you intend to go along the practical route then you should have enough adventure in your spirit to 'have-a-go'. Set out to find out. Ask people. Read the instructions on the tin. Be brave. Experience is invaluable, so get some. There have been many times when people have said to me "I like your tent, where did you get it made?" and when I say that I did it and it's my first attempt at sewing, they're surprised. You don't need skill, so much as patience. It's not a perfect tent. I know where all the little 'bodges' are, but that doesn't matter. As I'll say elsewhere, being 'amateur' is allowed. Let's take a look at the practicalities in some detail.

The Hull.

As with most small boats built in GRP at around this time the hull was made of chopped strand mat (CSM) and polyester resin. This is the simplest/cheapest GRP construction. More modern craft should use woven glass cloth and resins that are more water resistant. I was very lucky that after the prolonged immersion, my hull was not blistered by absorbing water, a process called osmosis. The inside of the hull had been painted white (or flowcoated) to slightly disguise the rougher inner face of the glass strand texture and this paint did flake away over the next few seasons, but I allowed it to do so. Eventually I repainted the interior to offer some weather protection to the exposed fiberglass.

50

Deck, side seats, thwart and centreboard were made either from solid mahogany or mahogany marine plywood and were remarkably undamaged by the water (which had been fresh), because they had been well maintained prior to immersion and although all their protective varnish was stripped off, it was possible to restore the colour and recoat them. Exposing the bare wood surface can often improve its colour if the wood is faded. Coating it with oxalic acid, then washing off again brings back the colour of mahogany. The timber least affected by exposure to the elements is teak, so it would be the timber of choice for new work, if it was available and could be afforded. In replacing the timber components in the hull I checked all their fixings and replaced old brass screws/bolts (many of which were 'wasted' through galvanic action), with the much more durable stainless steel, where possible.

I was most pleased that the plywood deck and natural timber rubbing strips around the gunwale did not require paint, for they were not disfigured by water staining, but could be re-varnished, for varnished wood has a warmth and 'life' not evident in paintwork. The later Torches have glass-moulded decks and although this is wonderful for reducing maintenance it means that they lack the character of a boat with a shiny wooden deck. As I have already hinted, I am a great believer in the merits of GRP for durability, water resistance, strength and saving maintenance, but I can appreciate the use of a restricted amount of wood for its warmth and beauty.

Buoyancy.
I had built-in buoyancy tanks at the bow and stern, which were sealed with 100mm circular, plastic access hatches to allow inspection and probably also intended to allow me to mop out any water which might find its way inside through these same hatches or the seams where the tanks were sealed to the hull. These tanks took up quite a large amount of space that I intended to use for storage so I purchased some larger access hatches and fitted them to the top of the tanks, initially leaving the old inspection hatches in place. These larger hatches transformed the storage available. In general, I use the larger bow tank for domestic items, galley equipment, food, sleeping bag and mattress etc. The smaller stern tank holds tools, ropes, boat spares, cleaning equipment etc. This affects the trim (fore and aft) of the boat. In general one should aim to store weight as centrally as possible so with restricted space,

water containers (heavy) need to be in the middle and sleeping bags (light) should be at the ends.

There is sometimes a mistaken belief that a buoyancy tank with something inside it has less 'buoyancy' but this is not really so. The weight of the contents has some effect on the overall weight of the boat to be supported, but the buoyant lift of the tank when immersed in water remains the same, providing it is still watertight. This is something that it is important to understand so I will quote directly from an explanatory DCA article as this illustrates how useful this bank of information can be.

Storage inside tanks.

Modified extract from a letter from David Fraser.

DCA Bulletin No. 82/08

Buoyancy and flotation are simply a matter of weight and volume; applying this to the situation of a capsized and waterlogged boat this statement must be modified by saying that what matters is only the immersed, underwater, volume of the boat, though it is the overall weight of the boat that counts here (together with the weight of the crew if they are on board rather than floating independently in the water beside the boat. To understand clearly the physics of the situation, imagine two identical boats in a capsized and waterlogged state; then add to each boat an identical load (same weight, same volume) they will float at exactly the same level EVEN THOUGH ONE OF THE LOADS WAS STOWED INSIDE THE BUOYANCY TANK AND THE OTHER WAS STOWED ELSEWHERE IN THE BOAT (but not underwater). This is because the total weight of each boat is equal to that of the other, and so is the immersed volume.

It is worth looking at the exception - a load (such as a sealed bag of clothes or sleeping bag) stowed not in a buoyancy tank but in a position where it will be underwater when capsized. In this case the load does contribute additional buoyancy (compared with a boat which has its load stowed out of the water). The extra buoyancy can be as great as 62.5 lbs for every cubic foot of the volume of the load. The only way that buoyancy can be destroyed is by ballasting the boat with 62.5 lbs of extra weight for every cubic foot of buoyancy.

Repairs to tanks.

It is important that buoyancy tanks are water resistant but experience shows that this cannot be assumed to be the case with small dinghies. How can you tell if your tanks leak? You can do the obvious things such as observe them over a period of time, or douse the seams with water. I have found that the most frequent causes of difficulty are the access hatches themselves, rudder fittings that penetrate into the stern tank or other fixings, screws or bolts for floorboard and seat securing. These can be cured by removing them and reseating them with new sealant being carefully and accurately positioned. If the seam that bonds the tank to the hull is suspected it might be tested. Most sailing clubs have someone with equipment for pressure testing buoyancy tanks in order to certify sailing craft for racing. If you cannot find such a person you will discover that with a bit of ingenuity you can do the job yourself. You can modify or replace an access hatch cover using plywood or a tin lid so that it has a cycle inner tube valve passing through it. Seal/secure it in place of the existing hatch cover using Plasticine, Blue Tack or putty and then 'inflate' the tank with a cycle pump. It is surprising how little pressure is necessary to reveal weaknesses in the bond of the tank to the hull. Len Wingfield 127/35 suggests blowing into a simple plastic tube rather than using a cycle valve, just like inflating a balloon. If a leak is found it will have to be repaired, probably using finely woven glass tape and epoxy resin. The area that the tape bonds to must be cleaned with abrasive paper first. The easiest way to buy small quantities of epoxy resin is in the form of twin tubes of glue from hardware shops. Many car spares shops will have glass cloths (but see the next paragraph below) for polyester bodywork repairs. Larger quantities will require a visit to chandlers.

It is worth knowing that most glass cloths are specifically made for use with polyester resin, relying upon it to soften a special 'binding dressing' to make them flexible. Epoxy resin usually will NOT do this, so for larger scale work it is worth checking that cloth and resin are compatible before investing too much money.

Additional buoyancy.
It is important to consider how your craft will behave if it should be capsized. Exercises at the sailing centre showed the Torch rear tank provided insufficient buoyancy at the stern. Later models used fore-and-aft side tanks instead, thus putting additional buoyant lift under the water. In earlier craft this lack of sufficient buoyancy could be remedied by attaching inflated bags beneath the side seats. If bags are applied they take up valuable space. Most cruising dinghies can use inflatable rollers, which are tough enough to assist in moving the boat across a beach to get it into or out of the water. Equipment like this is available through major chandlers.

I use a roller and a large yacht fender that provide some small buoyancy, to act as rollers and also fender the craft when in a marina. The long ties attached to the fender ends are used to secure them very firmly to the underside of the stern seats. If buoyancy is loose in a capsize, or free to float out it will be useless. It must remain immersed and in its position during capsize, when it exerts a great deal of pressure on its ties and also the seat fixings.

Floorboards and sleeping.
It might appear that the bit of boat that you stand on is of no special importance, but with an open cruising dinghy this is not the case. The type of flooring can have a direct bearing on potential suitability of a boat for cruising, because it will probably be the first choice location for sleeping. Many modern craft have no separate internal floorboards; the crew just stands on the inside of the hull. It saves weight and expense in manufacture. Some very new craft may have sealed internal mouldings which position the floor above the outside water level to make them self bailing but shallow inside. Prior to the introduction of these methods most craft had plywood panels set into internal mouldings and before that, dinghies had separately constructed plank floorboards attached to wedge shaped supports on their undersides.

The general requirement for a cruising dinghy is that the hull should have sufficient internal depth to offer some protection and to provide a relaxed natural seating position. If the crew intends to sleep on the floor then it will have to be wide enough to allow a person to lie beside the centreboard casing and there should be sufficient clearance under the thwart to allow a person to turn over without getting stuck. This is usually only possible in the bigger and beamier boats. The bed should also be (in the main) a level surface and as dry as possible. A very small amount of water in the bilge can travel a long way, so the bed must be elevated above the hull to allow for water that inevitably finds its way down to the bilge. Many modern craft, as mentioned above, pose problems in this area. Smaller, narrower boats will have to arrange a bed (or beds) at the height of the thwart. This problem, of where the bed will be situated must be an early consideration, because it will not be guaranteed that a large flat area can be found, and the shorter the boat becomes, the harder it may be to find the space.

In my case, my old fashioned Torch had four separate planked floorboard structures, but the clearance below the thwart was too small to allow sleeping with them in their normal place.

When I removed the rear two I discovered that with some modification they could be dropped into place to bridge the gap from the rear buoyancy tank to the thwart, filling the gap between the side seats. When they were both in place they made a flat platform 1880 long x 1370 wide (6ft 2ins x 4ft 6ins) amidships. This is the largest sleeping area that I have ever had on any boat that I have owned. In fact, I found that in practice I needed only one floorboard to be lifted and lodged in place when cruising by myself. This creates the advantage of allowing me to sit on the long side of my 'bunk' with my feet on the other (normally positioned) floorboard and an even greater advantage of providing an accessible, large temporary storage area beneath the raised bunk-floorboard for some of the sailing or domestic gear which must be taken out of the forward buoyancy tank when 'living' aboard, plastic bags of food and supplies in particular.

The floorboards will need to be strong enough to support the weight of an adult sitting on them if they are acting as a bridge in this way because originally they were designed for the hull of the boat to support them. Plywood floorboards are often too large to start moving around and too flexible to span areas unless they are supported all around. In the Mirror dinghy the plywood daggerboard is usually used, along with an additional piece of ply to form the basis of the bunk, by covering the sunken foot well.

Whatever arrangement is used it is very important that the floorboards are firmly secured in place, when sailing, in case of capsize. Although my boat had been sailed for years as a training craft and I had engaged in leisure sailing in her for further years, nobody in all that time had ever given real thought to fixing the floorboards in place. There is a very valuable account by John Baden in DCA Bulletin 97 of a capsize in his Drascombe Lugger on Christchurch Ledge in gathering darkness. During the account he says this *'various items were just floating about, in particular the floorboards which were a nuisance as they impeded our movements in the cockpit of the boat.'* One of his major conclusions afterwards was the following *'One thing I intend to do for the future is to tie the floorboards down because they were a real nuisance when they floated up and we had to let them float away; had they been tied down it would have been easier to do what we had to do and they would have also provided more buoyancy; the locker lids also tended to float away with the air underneath them, but these we managed to re-attach.'* It is worth noting that John Baden concludes (of this very popular cruising craft, having been rescued by the lifeboat) *'I do not think it would have been possible to bail out the boat as she was so deep in the water.'* Perhaps there is a lesson here that one should not assume that just because a boat is popular and sold commercially, you should not check it over thoroughly for yourself, according to your own criteria. Once you are on the water, you will be responsible for your own and other people's safety. <u>You have to start thinking for yourself.</u>

Fastening down floorboards means that they in their turn can be used to secure other equipment. In my boat, in normal sailing conditions, the floorboards hold in place the anchor and its warp, the water container(s) and the oars.

To secure the floorboards I glassed wooden securing blocks (see below) in strategic positions. Some formed ledges overlapping the top edges of the boards and others had 9mm plywood turn buttons screwed onto their tops to allow the boards to be released and removed for maintenance or for access for cleaning beneath them. It usually only takes one family picnic to deposit pebbles, sand and various sandwich contents into the bilge.

Securing floorboards.

The most usual method is to secure wooden blocks to the hull and then to add turn buttons to them. In order to do this, experiment with blocks to determine whether they are the right shape, similarly with the turn buttons. They do not have to be a uniform shape.

To secure the blocks in position.

Clean the inside of the hull and roughen with glasspaper. The wooden blocks can be glued in place using epoxy resin and then their location checked for floorboard insertion and removal. The wooden blocks need to be shaped so as to allow the glass to take up the correct shape and adhere to both the block and the hull. Fillets of polyester resin putty (sometimes called car body filler) can be used to round the corners where the blocks meet the hull. Polyester resin and chopped strand mat can then be used to do the securing. When the glass has set it can be trimmed, smoothed and painted over to blend with the hull colour. In the event of the failure of the bond of the new glass to the old glass of the hull it can still be repaired. It may be re-bonded with epoxy resin (*available as glue in twin tube packs*). See chapter 5 for my sleeping arrangements.

Decisions. Decisions.

If you have chosen a boat for cruising, how will you arrange the sleeping? If you already have one, have you tried lying down aboard to test the comfort of the likely sleeping position?

The Centreboard / centreplate / daggerboard.
The hull has a couple of vitally important additions, sub-systems upon which the greater system depends, the centre/daggerboard and the rudder.
The centreboard is the most popular device used in dinghies for providing lateral resistance, but some craft such as the Mirror 10 use a daggerboard. As mentioned earlier this can foul the kicking strap when raised. Long-term dinghy cruisers have been known to modify the rig to lift the boom higher to avoid this, or have changed boards for the heavier more complex, centreboard structure. (DCA Bull. 81, John Gray. David McClellan. Skipper 14. Bull. 86.)

Centreboards pose their own problems. Essentially with the lightweight approach to open dinghy cruising if a damage problem arises, or the board gets jammed with stones, it is usually possible to get ashore, then roll the boat onto its side, to gain access to attend to the difficulty (using a sail batten?). If the board is in fact a plate that is made from metal to add ballast weight, it could be a different story. Lifting equipment may be needed unless the plate can be accessed from inside the boat, preferably whilst it is still afloat. There are systems that allow this, but they are not common, because they cost a little more initially than the simple way of just drilling a hole right through the casing and putting a pivot bolt in it. If you were to build your own boat, this problem 'pivot bolt accessible whilst afloat' should be high on the list of design priorities. Beyond a certain point, carrying significant ballast in **open dinghies** begins to pose the question, Why? This is perhaps a contentious subject for debate, best dealt with elsewhere, for now.

The early Torches had galvanised centreplates, but I saw one that had problems when it forcibly ran aground and slightly bent the plate so that it could not be retracted into its narrow, board box. In some special cases lead can be attached to centreboards. (DCA Bull. 91. John Perry) I have seen Wayfarers modified for heavy centreplates, but they then required the addition of a winching system or tackle to raise them.

I have a simple plywood board that I extract and varnish well once a season. The boat has to be rolled onto its side to remove the board. As the boat is normally stored ashore the board remains lightweight (they can absorb water if left permanently afloat), dry and stiff. It is wedged into different positions by use of a compressed piece of hosepipe and the occasional use of an elastic shockcord loop when fully down. It can be pinned in the 'fully raised' position for security when trailing.

Later I will describe how I discovered that the loading limit of my boat is determined by the water level in the centreboard case. My voluminous little craft can manage to take the full family and all camping gear with additional shore tents etc. Under such a load it continues to sail well, even though it feels like a keelboat, but when going to windward or in wave conditions the water begins to splash in over the top of the casing as the water level inside it is so high. Whilst it can be baled out, it is not a good idea to sail far in this condition, which is a clear indicator that the boat is overloaded.

The Rudder.

I have the most popular dinghy rudder design, which is a pivoting plywood blade (see below) swinging between the plywood cheeks

of the rudderstock. The blade is pulled up and down with bits of string and elastic. I do not like this design and would not use it on anything but a slow dinghy. The main problem is guaranteeing that the blade is held right down, as the downhaul usually incorporates elastic shockcord to allow emergency movement as a safety precaution if the blade should hit an obstruction. Even under ordinary sailing loads the blade tends to move backwards. As it does so it becomes less efficient making the steering feel heavier. Inexperienced sailors rarely identify this fault. If the blade cannot be secured down or raises itself up during sailing it is subject to greater loads that can snap the blade. It is vulnerable on or near the shore especially if the boat is moved backwards. If the elastic is removed and the blade locked down, sometimes with thin dowel or a wing nut on the pivot bolt so that it cannot drift up, then the whole purpose of this design may be defeated. Being able to pivot the blade completely clear of the water like the one in the photograph is very good when living aboard.

I prefer a daggerboard rudder with the blade angled forwards, but not secured down. It is much more efficient and I have found (on other craft) that it will come up on gradual contact with the bottom in shallowing water. My only problem is aesthetic. This daggerboard rudder type looks efficiently modern; more at home on a catamaran and out of keeping with my wooden-gaffed craft, so I continue with the standard model, despite not liking it. This shows how one may choose to compromise. Functional efficiency is not everything. Keep an open mind and make your own choices.

Whatever rudder is used it is vitally important to ensure that it is strong enough and the pivot fittings are bolted onto the boat. When I rescued my boat from its years of immersion I found that many metal fittings were badly corroded by galvanic action. The brass screws just crumbled away. It was expensive, but it was essential to replace them with stainless steel throughout, including a stainless pivot bolt.

Rudder blades are often made of plywood with the visible wood grain arranged vertically. This means that some internal layers of wood are arranged horizontally and they will have little resistance to the major sideways force exerted by the water on the blade. This force is most concentrated along the edge of the bottom of the rudderstock cheeks. A plywood rudder blade (and also the centreboard) should have its visible grain running at 45 degrees to its vertical edges so that all the layers take their part in resisting the major force. The best wooden blades are built from vertical strips of solid timber bonded together. Their integrity will only be as good as the glue used to attach the strips to each other.

Tiller.
My tiller is a piece of simple, straight ash located into the stock and locked with a large split pin, attached to it (not the rudder) with a short length of line. This tiller was adequate when sailing fully crewed but when I sailed alone I needed an extension in order to get my own weight further forward in the boat. The extension needed a universal joint, also a simple way to locate it on the tiller. Later I found it necessary to have a way to fix the helm and initially I used pieces of string or elastic until I saw other DCA skippers using a helm-impeder as described in DCA Bull. No 86 by John Huntingford. This is an excellent device, simple to make with several possible variations. It cannot be too highly recommended. It has transformed my ability to manage the boat alone and I would rate it an essential piece of equipment for dinghy cruising.

For an even simpler arrangement capable of similar control see T. Jones 139/07. Just occasionally when the boat has to run for some distance and I want to be looking forward with my weight more central I have steered with lines attached to the tiller, as using the extension is not easy when it is aligned in-line straight forward.
I simply take a string of sufficient length and fold it halfway. At this point I make the double loops of a clove hitch, which is dropped onto the tiller end with the extension folded back. The lines go out to the rowlocks on the gunwale and back in to either hand. I sit

Details of John Huntingford's Helm Impeder.

Extremely simple to make, it allows locking pressure to be varied on the tiller but always allows instant movement of the tiller.

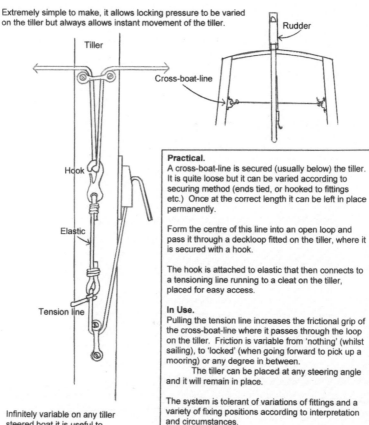

Tiller

Rudder

Cross-boat-line

Hook

Elastic

Tension line

Infinitely variable on any tiller steered boat it is useful to reduce 'sailing load' (weather helm), on cruising yachts.

Practical.
A cross-boat-line is secured (usually below) the tiller. It is quite loose but it can be varied according to securing method (ends tied, or hooked to fittings etc.) Once at the correct length it can be left in place permanently.

Form the centre of this line into an open loop and pass it through a deckloop fitted on the tiller, where it is secured with a hook.

The hook is attached to elastic that then connects to a tensioning line running to a cleat on the tiller, placed for easy access.

In Use.
Pulling the tension line increases the frictional grip of the cross-boat-line where it passes through the loop on the tiller. Friction is variable from 'nothing' (whilst sailing), to 'locked' (when going forward to pick up a mooring) or any degree in between.
The tiller can be placed at any steering angle and it will remain in place.

The system is tolerant of variations of fittings and a variety of fixing positions according to interpretation and circumstances.

The tiller can be totally released from the device by unhooking the tension line.

The rudder could be at either end of the diagram, but in general it would be at the lower end.

centrally, forwards of the thwart. It only takes a second to rig or discard, greatly reducing the effort of steering this particular course.

Safety Checking.
To daysail a boat, is quite different from cruising in it. It is wise to look closely at boards and steering during refurbishment and before going sailing with these questions in mind.

Decisions. Decisions.
In a capsize can the rudder, tiller or board detach and float away?
Will a metal plate forcibly drop back in its box if the boat is inverted?
How is the grain of the plywood arranged in the thin rudder blade?
Are there compression marks across the face of a plywood blade or board level with the bottom of the rudder stock cheeks, or hull?
Floorboards, will they float away?
Steering, is it adequate? Will it break?
Is the tiller strong and firmly attached to the rudder?
Are the rudder fittings bolted or screwed onto the hull?
What are the oarlocks/rowlocks made of? (Plastic isn't acceptable.)
You do not have to be an ancient mariner to know what the answers to these questions should be. If you do not find the right answers with your equipment, you should tackle the problems that you have found. Never ignore a problem and hope that it will go away or that it won't matter. It is up to you to respond to the challenge and work out a practical solution. If you cannot, then ask somebody else what they think. It's worth knowing that the DCA has a 'Technical Officer' just itching to prove his inventiveness.

Check existing arrangements.
The hull of the boat is the fundamental unit that carries all the systems. How well is it fitted for the cruising purpose (as opposed to pottering or occasionally racing in home waters with safety boat back up)? As soon as you cast off, will you find yourself in a position such as I did in this story?

Mirror, Mirror on the water.
I got into a borrowed Mirror dinghy for a quick whiz around the anchorage in fairly gusty conditions on tidal water, taking a relative beginner as crew to give them a joyride. I made only superficial checks. I was sailing away from the shallows pulling on the rudder blade downhaul when, with a twang, the rope came loose in my hand. I had little steering as the rudder blade was out of the water. No time for investigations, it was imperative to find a vacant buoy

amongst the moored cruisers that wind and tide were driving us down onto. Luck was on my side as I managed to grab a buoy as we passed. I hauled it forwards and prepared to secure the boat to the weedy rope. My first discovery was that I had no fairlead at the bow; my second was that there was no cleat to secure to. I did the obvious thing and took a turn of the mooring rope around the base of the mast. All the halliard cleats were fixed onto the mast at deck level (where the mast was stepped) so there was no alternative but to lock all the halliards to the mast with the mooring rope, so that now, the sails wouldn't come down. I tried to pull up the daggerboard to reduce the tidal drag, but it hit the kicking strap and was further restricted by contact with the boom.

I inspected the rudder to find that a single screw into the edge of the thin plywood blade had secured the downhaul. It couldn't be refastened. The blade uphaul was tied through a hole at the back of the rudder blade, a more secure design solution. At least I had oars and rowlocks (which I had checked before leaving) to get me back to the shore, but the oarlocks were plastic. These plastic devices should not be allowed on a boat. They are too weak and can snap off. They are my definition of 'a gear failure waiting to happen at the moment of greatest crisis', but I used them with caution and we did make it back.

Safety by design.

All the 'hardware' difficulties I faced in a brief five minutes on the water had basic design errors at their heart. I did not identify them, because the boat looked OK and my checks were superficial glances. I was at fault in this. This was an old boat, a wooden boat and a type where many of the craft have been amateur built. I should have been more wary. This dinghy class is one of the most popular to be found. Tens of thousands are sailed and raced. In general terms they may be satisfactory for what they do, but cruising is a different game and it demands subtle changes to the way a craft is arranged. Simply putting the halliard cleats a little higher on the mast would have allowed the possibility of securing the mooring warp. Having a fairlead and a strong cleat would have been even better. The boat's painter wasn't easily available as it was attached to the boat through a ring close to water level on the outside of the bow... but that's yet another design fault on these craft from the viewpoint of the cruising sailor.

I cannot stress this too highly. Living in an open dinghy means ironing out all the little problems and idiosyncrasies that are to be found on any craft, but which can usually be ignored or worked around when they are infrequently met on short day trips. If anything can go wrong, it will go wrong, so the safety of both crew and craft has to take a higher priority than normal when practically converting a boat for cruising.

Engines and all that....

Having a sound basic hull with strong well-positioned fittings is the basic requirement of the cruising dinghy, but as we move towards the sails which will power it, there is another fundamental decision to be made. Will you be using an engine?

The answer to this is of crucial importance, because it will tend to shape the kind of cruising that you will be involved in and even the kind of craft that you will choose to use. At this time I do not have an engine on my cruising dinghy, but it is equipped to take one, and if I should change the way that I cruise, then I would use one. I had better explain further.

If I should mention that I've NOT got an engine on my boat some sailors may instantly jump to their own conclusions. They may tell me how they too agree with me that engines are noisy, smelly abominations. That they too prefer not using them and sometimes wish they'd never been invented. I usually listen, but sooner or later I have to let slip that this is the reverse of my general thinking. There is no need for engines to be especially noisy or smelly these days and when it comes to using them, I enjoy their convenience, if I have one aboard.

Now this is the crux of the issue, so it's worth repeating, ... if I have one aboard... With an engine I find that I have a different approach to sailing from when I have not got one. I should say from the outset that I have a choice, due to the nature of my boat. My dinghy is relatively small and lightweight and can be rowed easily. When I embark on a journey I don't fight the tide and if the wind should fail I know I must use muscle rather than mechanics, so the distances I choose to undertake are governed by this requirement and are 'within the time available'. My little boat suits what I do, which is to sail mainly in sheltered water. It is very maneuverable and has minimal draught so that it can exploit the lightest puffs and chance the shallows, should the currents not be totally favourable. Many of my options are not available to even slightly larger or heavier craft. They have an engine because in these modern sailing times it would be almost irresponsible not to have one. If I decided to do more coastal cruising or frequently met commercial traffic then

I would probably need a more rugged craft with a permanently deployed engine.

I will widen this to temporarily speak about all sailing boats including the bigger cruisers. Engines have become an integral part of the way that most people now sail and keep their boats safe. The leisurely way of sail-when-the-wind-is-right is no longer an option for most people who have places to go and deadlines to meet. Our rivers and estuaries are rarely unobstructed sailing waters and the owners of the many moored craft which define the navigable channel by lining either side of it, reasonably expect that craft of any dimensions will not collide with their possessions through lack of motive power, even when the wind falls light. Insurance companies want to know about engines before accepting risk and the excess power that engines supply is now commonly harnessed to make available all manner of additional equipment which has become a commonplace necessity aboard modern craft.

Engines are common on seagoing dinghy cruisers.

I have nothing against engines for the majority of modern sailors. I recognise that there will always be a dedicated few who are religiously opposed to mechanical propulsion, but let them only once accept a tow and their zeal is surely undermined. No, I have nothing against engines, except, ... except ... the difference they can make in the minds of their owners.

My observation is that engines have taken patience away and with it, a significant part of sailing. There was a style of sailing where the lulls were tolerated equally with the gusts, when the sailor sat and contemplated what might have been or what was to come. The style included looking for wind shadows and trying to avoid them, as well as an appreciation of sitting still so as not to break the smoothness of the water flow whilst ghosting along. These are just a couple of things that seem now to be ebbing from the sail-cruising experience. The current fashion seems to be to hold to the sail through the first few minutes of the lull, but then if the wind doesn't return, or if movement does not pick up, the key will be turned or the cord pulled and the headsail rolled. Once the guaranteed progress of the engine establishes a yardstick for speed, it will stay on, even if the wind returns.

Sailing without an engine, there is no option. Knowing that it is the wind that is the motive power means patience is not being tested in the same way. Engineless sailors are not exercising patience. It only becomes patience when there is an engine and therefore, an easy option to increase speed; a choice to be made.

My primary reason for not having an engine in this particular boat, is that I have found it to be more relaxing. It determines the way that I sail. I plan ahead and try to get myself in the right place at the right time. It is an additional bonus that significant weight is saved and it doesn't need storage for engine and fuel (with the potential for smells and fire hazard). I'm not against being towed (I even carry a rope specially for this purpose), but I have found that this usually occurs when I am falling in with someone else's timetable rather than my own. I have protective plywood pads on my transom, so I'm prepared to use an engine when regulations insist upon it (e.g. certain inland waterways) but until then I continue to appreciate the natural sounds and having to exercise my ingenuity to propel myself from A to B in the relaxed manner that being engineless imposes.

Alternative mechanical power.
Petrol outboard power has long been accepted as the easiest way to mechanically power a cruising dinghy, but with environmental concern growing it may be that electric power will become more accepted. I do not want to enter the debate about how the electricity is generated, but I can say that I (elsewhere, for another purpose entirely) have a 10 watt Solar panel constantly battery charging and it does feel like 'clean and low cost' energy. The outstanding advantage of electric power, for me, is its quiet operation. I have made long journeys inland under oars and have felt pity for the many occupants of passing powerboats. I know that they really are missing out on the natural sounds of wind, reeds and birdsong. Rowing a dinghy makes me travel backwards and how nice it would be to be able to see where I am going; maybe an electric outboard?

The biggest immediate 'unknowns' when considering electricity are, the weight of the battery, followed by questions of speed and duration. I am not an expert so I was pleased to read a very informative account by George Saffrey (165/30) of his investigations and experiments with an electric outboard attached to his camping Cruz dinghy. He set out to answer all the layman's questions and he presented his conclusions totally without any jargon. I will extract from his article 'Silent Running'. His motor weighed about 7kgs (16lbs) and the battery 23.5 kgs (52lbs) from which he gets a theoretical range of 13naut. miles at 2.2 knots (on speed setting 3). At speed setting 5 his range would be 8 naut. miles at 3.1 knots. This furnishes us with some approximations that we can begin to visualize and we can see that for weekend camping/cruising the figures are 'interesting'. They become even more viable for anyone using ballasted boats where the batteries can be substituted for the ballast. With all that electric power and a solar panel, your dreams might begin to slide towards Navtex, echo sounder, lighting, sound systems, laptop, television and microwave, in other words all that dinghy cruising is supposed NOT to be about. One could go further and begin to behave like a world girdling solo sailor in the 'Roaring Forties', sobbing into your webcam, whilst you are actually somewhere on a canal in the West Midlands, but clearly, I am digressing. Electric power presents some interesting options. There is an electric boat association and their journal is called 'Electric Boat News'. Both of these might be good starting points for anyone interested in investigating alternative propulsion. (See 'Contacts' at the end of the book.)

Rowing.
I mentioned earlier that my Torch dinghy was relatively narrow when compared with some sailing dinghies. This was because the designer Bert Keeble wanted it to be used for teaching rowing as well as sailing. Unusually for a sailing boat it originally had two rowing positions (see the illustration of 'Panda' in chapter 2). The result is that it is easy to row, whereas wider boats need progressively longer and longer oars or more elevated rowing positions to be effective, or they tend to use paddles instead of oars. Paddling is nowhere near as effective as rowing on wide, heavy craft that also need steering. Paddling such a craft against a tidal flow is almost ineffective; hence the popularity of small outboard motors on the wider cruising dinghies.

Without an engine the oars and oarlocks become of prime importance. They must not fail. The first rule for me (as you may know by now) is not to use plastic oarlocks. They are just not strong

enough. Longer oars can themselves pose stowage problems in many smaller dinghies. I have sufficient open access to lay them along either side of my centreboard case secured to the floorboards with clipped elastic. Many people use this method, fastening the oars to each other at the front and back of the casing. One or two people fasten them along the side decks outside the cockpit of the boat. Whatever system is used

Moving through moorings in light conditions.   they need to be accessible instantly especially if they are used for functions other than rowing (see sections on tents and sails) such as poling out sails, depth sounding etc.

There are times, if the wind falls light, when it becomes necessary to supplement sailing with rowing. The boat can be steered with one hand (or foot) on the tiller whilst rowing with a single oar. In rivers with wind shadows the conditions can alternate suddenly between flat calm and knockdown gusts so that oars have to be shipped rapidly as propulsion moves from oar to sail and back again. Getting oars in and out of oarlocks quickly is a problem, but a more annoying difficulty is the water running back along the loom of the oar and up your arm or into the boat.

4.

Sailing a Dinghy Cruiser.

DCA Quotes.

What sort of boat?
The biggest you can handle on shore, the smallest you can live on
and keep your gear dry... and...especially... a gunter rig.
Ted Jones.

4.
Sailing equipment.

Sailing.
There are two interlinked considerations when thinking of sailing a boat. The first is the way that the boat sails and the second is the sailing system itself, the rig and the sails. To some extent the first is governed by the second, but also it is influenced by all the factors which we have already dealt with, the components which make up the hull, its weight etc.

The way it sails.
The way the boat sails is of prime importance. Speed is not really the issue with cruising; it is more useful to have a degree of comfort when sailing for sustained periods of time. Going more slowly does not mean sailing inefficiently, it is more to do with matching the sail area to the undertaking. The activity is 'sailing sightseeing' and, during sailing, it is usual to engage in a variety of domestic activities, changing clothes, eating snacks, taking photographs and checking pilotage details to mention just a few. You do not want to have to be constantly jumping up and down to keep the boat from capsizing whilst occupied in this way. People have crossed the Channel on windsurfers and sliding-seat canoes, but this is probably not for the majority of 'mature' cruising dinghy sailor.

The reaction of the boat to gusts of wind should be predictable, steady and smooth. It should not be so tender that it instantly falls on its ear with each puff of breeze; there should be plenty of time to react. It helps if the boat will gently follow the wind in the puffs, but still be easy to steer and not become so 'hardmouthed' that she will luff irrespective of what you do. Here is a relevant question. Could the boat be sailed with the sheets held in jamb cleats or with the helm impeder almost constantly engaged without undue risk of capsize?

Sailing Systems. The Mast.
Most masts these days are single, tall aluminium spars as this system provides durable, simple, lightweight efficiency. Their main problem is that they are rather long for road towing and putting them up and down needs good balance and strength. Gunter rigs basically split the mast in half, the lower section being the mast and the upper section being the gaff. Rigs using this principle are popular amongst cruising dinghy sailors because the spars will fit

inside the boat when travelling and they can be put up with little special physical effort. Once the rig is assembled it is very similar in appearance and performance to the Bermudian rig. When sailing in upriver locations the gunter may have the advantage, especially when shooting bridges, as only the gaff may need dipping temporarily, rather than taking down the whole mast.

A possible disadvantage of the standard gunter sail is that it can be limited in the amount of area that can be reefed out of it. The critical distance that restricts it is from the foot of the gaff, to the boom. The limit of easy reefing is found when the sail is eased to be tied down and these two points meet each other. To reef further can mean unfastening the sail from the spars if they are secured by lashings, as mine are. It can become an impossibly time-consuming process. It is possible to completely rearrange components of the mast, the gaff, the halliard and the sail attachment system to make it all reefable (J. S. Perry Bull. No 104. & D. Sumner Bull 208. describes such systems), but this was not an option for me as I wished to retain the essential arrangements of the craft I was using. (More rigging details are described in 'Rigging and Covers'.)

The Sails.

Visibility all round is essential for the sake of safety. With extended periods on the water and sailing in locations that are lesser known, there is less concentration on the actual process of sailing. You need to be able to relax and look around and not be caught out by unknown obstructions in a blind spot as the boat approaches them, so deck-sweeping headsails are probably to be avoided.

To achieve the right performance under a variety of sailing conditions is going to require a wide range of flexibility with the rig. I began with the ordinary, two sails designed for my boat. My main has 61sq.ft. and the little jib has 18sq. ft. The boat is not regarded as being fast.

I found that I could sail to about force 4 with full sail and then I needed to reef. This is done by lowering the sail and tying in reef points, taking the main's area down to about 36 sq. ft. With this I could go to the lower end of force 6 in sheltered water, but would not be comfortable if the wind was gusting. I never forget that the scariest moments usually come when running, over canvassed, in an increasing wind. I think that this describes the fairly typical performance for most dinghies using their plain sails. It is adequate for local sailing, but it may need to be extended for real cruising

Decisions, Decisions.

It should be mentioned that reefing whilst afloat is a process that requires practice. Many dinghy sailors may never have 'hove-to' in their boat, or dropped the main, tied in a reef and then re-hoisted it. Many sails need extra rope to tie down the luff tack and clew outhaul (which must be tied DOWN as well as pulled OUT), some need alternative kicking strap arrangements or the halliard re-fixing. What do you do with the jib during the process of main reefing? Letting it flog is not a good idea. Will it be on a roller luffspar? Can you reach across the foredeck to pull the jib down the forestay or will an extra downhaul be needed? Can you reef the jib? Do the jib sheets need to have a different lead? This book is not trying to teach sailing, but it is important to point out that having the right sails is of limited use unless the process of changing them has been worked through and all the inevitable 'bugs' ironed out of the systems not only in the dinghy park, but also out on the water.

Dropping the jib may reduce sail area, but may result in the loss of control of the boat when going about. Will the boat go to windward in heavy weather and tack reliably under main alone or jib alone? This is a question that can only be answered from practical experiment and experience. Another perhaps even more important question is whether the boat will run safely under reefed sails with a strong wind and a following sea. The chances are that this limitation will be the first one to be discovered. Many dinghies are vulnerable to broaching when running, as the area of the main can overpower the smaller jib.

The easy answer to most of these problems is to reef the main down to an appropriate size, but in so doing, the sail tends to lose shape and become less effective. I found a particular problem with my boat because I was using a gunter rig and I could not reef the main further than its normal single reef. At this point the gaff contacted the boom. (One-line reefing. Len Wingfield 127/34)

Reefing the sliding-gunter main.

For some time I had been aware that I didn't have a quick method for reefing my Torch. It had the simplest systems that it is possible to have and I didn't want to complicate them. I didn't want to start screwing lots of modern hardware onto the boat. I wanted it to remain essentially the same, uncluttered... BUT ... when you need to reef and you don't reef, because it's going to be difficult and take too long, then it's time to think again, or sooner or later, you're going to be scared, very scared. So you wait until you are ... and then you look at it, seriously.

When I started thinking about the problem, this was what I found was needed to reef my boat. I hadn't broken the process down before, because I was probably too lazy, or I was avoiding the issue. To reef, I had to lower the sail into the boat and re-hoist it again upon completion. This was the situation.

1. The main halliard was tied onto the gaff at different locations according to the sail area required, defined by small wooden wedges screwed onto the gaff. To reef the sail the gaff was dropped, the halliard untied and moved further up the gaff to the reef position to be retied (Rolling hitch 19/127)).

2. Extra pieces of separate 'string' were needed to tie down luff and leech.

3. One end of the several reefing ties that were threaded through cringles in the sail had to be passed under the foot of the sail to be tied to their opposite ends, each one in a reef knot.

This is the old fashioned, traditional, but utterly reliable standard practice. It works, but it is slow. It is best done by first sailing to the shore and then taking ten to fifteen minutes finding extra string, threading, tying and tensioning then testing it to see if it all sets correctly and is functioning well. Doing it afloat takes rather too much time unless you have a biggish piece of water and ample clearance to leeward. If you want to go to windward, you are going to lose an awful lot of distance that could take you an hour or more to make up, depending on conditions because, by definition, the elements will be against you when you are reefing.

I had always used this method on this boat because of simplicity and in relatively confined waters a riverbank is usually in the vicinity. I say, 'on this boat', because I have had other boats and used different systems on them, especially single-line reefing. This is a simple way to pull the luff and leech down and secure them. It immediately addresses action 2 above. It saves lots of finding, tying, threading and tensioning separate pieces of string, because the rope required is already there and fixed in the correct positions ready for use.

Systems such as this are accepted as standard these days, and used on many boats (see David Sumner 208/34). Incidentally, I have an added wrinkle that I use for the second reef (but not on my Torch as it has only a single reef capacity). I use snap hooks on the ends of the reefing line that are not passed through the cringles on the sail. The line has enough length to unfasten the clips and re-clip them onto the reefing cringles of the second reef as the sail is eased away. This avoids the necessity of duplicating the whole system, which involves hanging lots of different coloured lines from the sail for each reef, a system that is sometimes seen on yachts.

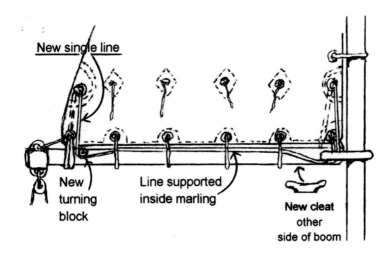

When I came to apply the system to my dinghy I thought that I would have to attach some fittings like plastic fairleads on the boom to support the reefing line to stop it from falling too low. When I actually started work on it I immediately saw that the old fashioned way my main is attached to its spars by 'marling', that is, lashing it to the boom with a continuous thin rope, gave me the chance of threading the reefing line inside this securing rope to stop it from being draped across the cockpit. Also, I didn't have to use a fixed cheek block to turn it upwards from the boom to the tack reef point in the sail, as I have wooden gaff jaws already drilled with holes to take the securing lashings for the sail and there was sufficient room for the addition of another line through these holes. To secure the end of the line at the front of the boom I used a small horn cleat on the boom (wooden to be unobtrusive, that I made myself), so that my complete single-line system was on the boom. It could be also secured to the mast, but I remove the whole boom/gaff/sail from the mast when making up my tent, so keeping everything on the boom made it easier for me. There is friction within the system, but this turned out to be advantageous. I can grasp the reefing line halfway along the boom and pull it. This reefs the clew. I can then move to the front of the boom and pull the tack down as a separate action. Whilst I do this, the clew reef does not fall out. This gives me the freedom to handle the kicking strap and the main halliard whenever I want to, within the whole process. Problem 2 was sorted.

I had produced this first part of the system by adding only one turning block for the clew and one wooden horn cleat for fixing the end of the reefing line, so I was rather pleased at the simplicity of the conversion. I knew that once the tack and clew were secured the sail was effectively reefed, but the sail would not set efficiently until the reef points across the sail were pulled in and tied. If this was not done, the fullness of the belly of the sail meant that it wasn't flat enough to sail properly in heavy wind.

Tying separate reef points always takes quite some time to do. It is possible to have a single line passing through them all, but it becomes miles long and is difficult to loosen when shaking the reef out. I considered the existing individual reefing ties. The problem was in finding the loose end of the tie underneath, on the opposite side of the sail and then tucking it through, under the bottom edge of the sail. This was time consuming. I had always been told not to tie these reefing pennants around the boom, but to make sure that they went under the boltrope which only adds to the time. Looking at the hoisted sail I suddenly saw a solution.

Quick-tie reefing pennants.

The reefing ties through the sail had been put on by the sailmaker. They are the same length on either side of the sail and they stay in place because they have a knot tied in them on either side of the sailcloth. I noticed that their positions across the sail happened to coincide with the cringles along the foot of the sail that held the rope securing the sail to the boom with the marling. I untied a reefing pennant by taking out its knots. I tied a stopper knot right at one end and

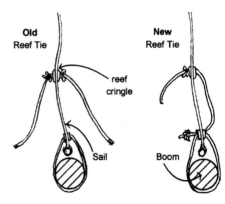

threaded it through the marling-cringle <u>at the foot of the sail</u> immediately below its reefing-cringle. I took it up the other side of the sail and threaded it back through the reefing cringle. I checked it was not tight enough to crease the sail cloth and tied another securing knot close to the cloth so that the pennant still had a loose end, long enough to tie the reef into the sail.

It sounds complicated to write, but this simple adjustment of the lengths of the two sides of the reefing pennant, totally solved the problem of finding the loose end and passing it under the sail. Both ends are now passed through cringles and appear on the same side of the sail. One is dangling from the sail in the usual place; its opposite end is a knot appearing from the sail cringle close to the boom below it. Now I can find and tie all pennants in less than 30 seconds, or do it at a convenient time whilst the sail is set, if I wish. I had solved problem 3 with the equipment that was already there. I'd just rearranged it.

Re-fixing the halliard to the gaff.

The biggest problem had been saved until last. I wanted to avoid dropping the gaff right into the boat, untying the halliard, moving it up the gaff and retying it. This is a problem that has long occupied the minds of some of the best gunter-rig sailors, such as John Perry 104/06 and Howard Morgan 209/41. I'll digress slightly to say that John's total article is probably the best piece of cruising dinghy design analysis that can be found and I cannot recommend it too highly. Read it. Howard's much more recent contribution has the best-annotated colour photographs of all the parts that I have mentioned. David Sumner 208/34 recently won the DCA's Peter's Pint (technical) trophy for his account of exactly how he addressed this same reefing difficulty, amongst several other modifications to his Mirror. I didn't refer to any of these pieces as I wanted to totally understand the difficulties and find an answer from first principles, so my solution evolved slightly differently due to my individual circumstances, but it has similarities with each, as we were all addressing the same questions. I had the original wooden spars for my boat and didn't want to drill new holes, or add new fittings to the middle of my gaff, especially as it is the ridge pole for my tent and when being so used, it goes into a snug-fitting bag with the mainsail attached. I also wished to avoid having to fit a second halliard to my mast (to lift the heel of the gaff).

These things take a 'Mastermind's-worth' of thinking around all the different options and evaluating each one in detail, but in the end I sorted it out with one small cleat attached to the gaff jaws, two bits of rope with thimbled-eyes spliced in one end, and the gaff basically untouched. This was my solution.

Practical Dinghy Cruiser

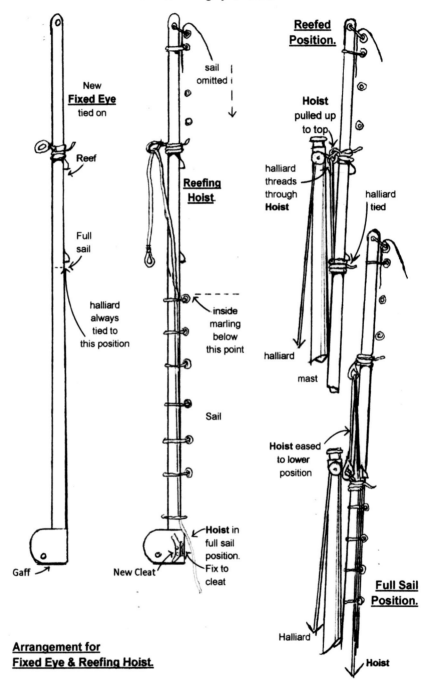

New
Fixed Eye
tied on

Reef

Full
sail

halliard
always
tied to
this position

Gaff

**Arrangement for
Fixed Eye & Reefing Hoist.**

sail
omitted

**Reefing
Hoist.**

inside
marling
below
this point

Sail

Hoist in
full sail
position.
Fix to
cleat

New Cleat

Hoist
pulled up
to top

halliard
threads
through
Hoist

halliard
tied

halliard

mast

Hoist eased
to lower
position

**Full Sail
Position.**

Halliard

Hoist

One Fixed-eye rope (length about 1m. or 3ft) is lashed to the spar just above the reefed-position wedge on the gaff with a rolling hitch. As it is a rope attachment, the spar is not damaged and it also allows the eye to have a universal hinging movement. It will be used to hold the halliard to the gaff in the reefed position.

This next section will sound complicated and needs to be checked against the diagram.

A longer Reefing-Hoist rope (about 4m or 12ft in my case, with the eye on its upper end.) passes through this Fixed-rope eye. It has to be long enough for the top end with the loop to reach down to the lowest halliard attachment point on the gaff. Its tail end goes up and through the fixed-eye loop, then right down the gaff to secure to a cleat at the gaff jaws, so it can be reached by the crew from inside the boat. Once this reefing-hoist tail passes the normal halliard securing point on its way down the gaff, it can be led inside the gaff marling to stop it from loosely flapping about until it reaches the cleat at the jaws.

Both of these ropes remain on the gaff at all times and are virtually invisible as they are well tucked away. In practice, under normal sail, they can be ignored and they are totally unobtrusive. They are just there for when they are needed.

Attaching the main halliard to the gaff by tying it does not change, except that it is first threaded through the eye of the Reefing-hoist rope and it is then tied to the gaff in the normal (full sail) place in the normal way with its rolling hitch. The sail is hoisted and set normally. The point where the main halliard is tied to the gaff will not need to be moved during reefing.

To move the securing point of the halliard to the gaff on the hoisted main, loosen the main halliard, only a couple of feet. The gaff will fall away from the mast at the top. Take up tension by pulling on the Reefing-hoist line and secure it to its cleat on the gaff jaws. This pulls the gaff back in, towards with the mast at the top. The point where the halliard is now secured to the gaff is effectively at the place where previously it was tied in the reefed position. This takes about 15 seconds.

Reversing the process when shaking the reef out is even quicker as the weight of all the parts, work to release the system. The hardest part is re-hoisting the main after readjusting the kicking strap. Total reefing time from sailing to sailing again (including adjust halliard positions and pull in, then secure single line) is about

45 seconds; with reef pennants tied in, it probably takes about a minute and a half? Practice could improve this. Having put this off for years and having suffered moments of deep discomfort and even fear as a result, I now wish that I tackled it sooner, because the answer turned out to be fairly straightforward, additional kit minimal and final result, a relief.

I have the lines operating on the port side of the rig and so it is desirable to be on that tack when making adjustments, so that all fixing points are visible. With more thought I might have placed it on the starboard side to put me on the right-of-way tack when I was engaged in the reefing process. I have to stand up when reaching up the gaff, but this is the penalty I pay for having the total system on the rig rather than on the mast. Marking the halliard with the two hoist positions, speeds up the process.

Reefed sailing.
Sailing reefed does not always mean that the weather is bad. Here, I am not concentrating on sailing the boat, so the sails are free and boat in on the helm impeder. This picture was taken before the reefing modifications just described were added. Note. I **do** have a buoyancy aid on. It is tricky to see, because I always prefer to wear it underneath my sailing jacket.

Heavy weather.
However, the first priority is to make the boat handle in very heavy weather if possible. This is not because there is any intention to go out seeking strong conditions, but it is to provide the peace of mind of knowing that should the boat be caught out, there will be a sailing option available to get the boat to a safe position. Whilst it is possible to reduce sail by dropping the main this may then mean that the boat will only sail off the wind. This is a dangerous option, because it will inevitably mean being driven towards the lee shore. If the boat can retain some windward ability there will be the option of seeking the

safer shelter of the windward shore or working the boat across the wind. A vital lesson to be appreciated in sailing is that a boat will not go to windward without sail up.

Storm Mainsail.

My decision was to make up a storm mainsail system for 'emergency' use. I could see that the normal sailing system would suffice for all but the most extreme circumstances, so it was only necessary to have a heavy weather sail for very rare occasions, that might almost never happen. Its area was determined by the

Heavy Weather Sail. No Scale.

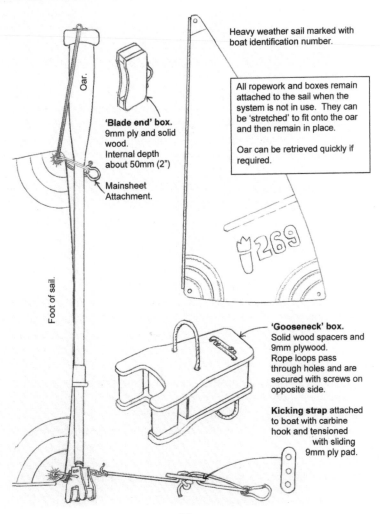

Oar.

'Blade end' box.
9mm ply and solid wood.
Internal depth about 50mm (2")

Mainsheet Attachment.

Foot of sail.

Heavy weather sail marked with boat identification number.

All ropework and boxes remain attached to the sail when the system is not in use. They can be 'stretched' to fit onto the oar and then remain in place.

Oar can be retrieved quickly if required.

'Gooseneck' box.
Solid wood spacers and 9mm plywood.
Rope loops pass through holes and are secured with screws on opposite side.

Kicking strap attached to boat with carbine hook and tensioned with sliding 9mm ply pad.

mast length, with the foot of the sail being shaped by proportion. It has an area of 18 sq ft. The construction is described in the sketch illustration. It fits into a small bag and it weighs about 1kg in total. The concept was to remove the normal mainsail with the boom and gaff to which the sail is lashed. Then hoist a small main only as high as the mast alone. A replacement boom was needed so rather than carry a spare spar I made up two specially shaped 'boxes' to fit on either end of an oar and added rope loops for the attachment of main tack, clew outhaul, kicking strap and mainsheet. I used the normal mainsheet that attaches by using carbine hooks, but I had to add additional anchorage points further forward in the boat to enable the whole mainsheet system to be re-positioned. The sail was made from the top of an old cruiser sail that I cut down to size. I retained the luffrope, headboard and top batten. It was very important to apply extra tabling to the tack and the clew and to over sew the cringles, as this sail would only be used in strong wind conditions.

In actual use in relatively sheltered water at about force six, surprisingly I found myself to be a little under-canvassed in the lulls, but reasonably comfortable in the gusts. I found it tricky operating what was essentially a centre main arrangement, but the system did work and I was pleased that I had it.

Light wind sailing.
Having taken care of heavy weather I next turned my attention to lighter airs. A sail with increased area is much more likely to be used than a heavy weather sail. This is made possible due to choices based upon the weather forecasting systems. I found myself particularly in need of more sail area when the wind dropped off and I was running against an adverse tidal stream.

The easiest sail to go for is a spinnaker, but it is limited to running downwind unless it is cut flat and can be tensioned down the luff, when it might be described as a 'genniker'. I preferred this genniker type of sail; more of a genoa than a spinnaker, as I have noticed that one rarely gets a dead run for long periods of time in rivers and estuaries due to the weaving-about nature of the channel or obstructions caused by other craft. You usually end up broad reaching more frequently than dead running.

The problem I had was that my short mast is stepped well forward in the boat and would allow only a small sail of limited luff length, hardly better than the existing sail. My solution was to fit a bowsprit (all details on the drawing), thus extending the luff length and angling it considerably, which provides extra sail lift at the bow when running. The construction diagrams illustrate the equipment I evolved, but I will add some general notes on the sail systems here.

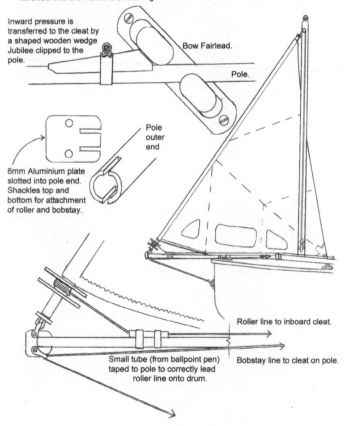

Bowsprit.
The sprit must be a stiff tube. I used a 20mm Aluminium tube with a thick (3mm) wall.

To hold the end down. A bobstay line is carbine hooked onto a fitting on the stem, passed through a shackle on the pole end then tensioned to a cleat on the inner end of the pole.

Pole is located in the bow fairlead. The inner end pushes into a drilled wooden pad screwed onto the front of the coaming frame.

Inward pressure is transferred to the cleat by a shaped wooden wedge Jubilee clipped to the pole.

Bow Fairlead.

Pole.

Pole outer end

6mm Aluminium plate slotted into pole end. Shackles top and bottom for attachment of roller and bobstay.

Roller line to inboard cleat.

Small tube (from ballpoint pen) taped to pole to correctly lead roller line onto drum.

Bobstay line to cleat on pole.

Roller Headsail System.
Roller Tube.
The basic idea was to use 22mm plastic overflow pipe as the tube. It needed joining about midway with a straight connector to make up its 3 metre length. I smoothed off the lower end of the top tube to

make it an easy fit into the connector. This allowed me to pull the joint apart even with the sail sleeved onto it, so that I could fold the rolled sail in half to make a parcel only 1.8 metres total length and no fatter than about 100mm for the combined assembly of sail, roller and bowsprit.

Headsail roller assembly.   Not to scale.

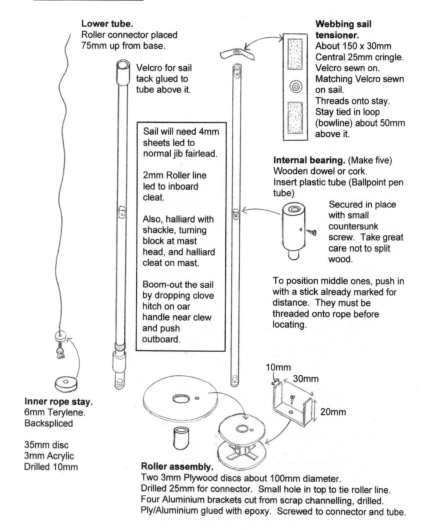

Lower tube.
Roller connector placed 75mm up from base.

Velcro for sail tack glued to tube above it.

Sail will need 4mm sheets led to normal jib fairlead.

2mm Roller line led to inboard cleat.

Also, halliard with shackle, turning block at mast head, and halliard cleat on mast.

Boom-out the sail by dropping clove hitch on oar handle near clew and push outboard.

Webbing sail tensioner.
About 150 x 30mm Central 25mm cringle. Velcro sewn on. Matching Velcro sewn on sail. Threads onto stay. Stay tied in loop (bowline) about 50mm above it.

Internal bearing. (Make five) Wooden dowel or cork. Insert plastic tube (Ballpoint pen tube)

Secured in place with small countersunk screw. Take great care not to split wood.

To position middle ones, push in with a stick already marked for distance. They must be threaded onto rope before locating.

10mm
30mm
20mm

Inner rope stay.
6mm Terylene. Backspliced

35mm disc
3mm Acrylic
Drilled 10mm

Roller assembly.
Two 3mm Plywood discs about 100mm diameter. Drilled 25mm for connector. Small hole in top to tie roller line. Four Aluminium brackets cut from scrap channelling, drilled. Ply/Aluminium glued with epoxy. Screwed to connector and tube.

Roller Drum.
This is a straight pipe connector with its internal web filed away for the basis of the roller drum and a couple of thin plywood discs.

Luff Tension.
When the sail is being folded it cannot be tensioned along its luff, but it must have some tension during sailing. This tension will pull the tubes together at the joint. The sail is secured to the tube at the sail tack with a Velcro flap. To tension it, the head of the sail is pulled upwards and secured with a Velcro webbing strap across the top of the tube. To ensure this remains in contact under load I usually add a couple of turns of tape around the webbing strap.

Bearings.
Very simple components act as bearings to allow the assembled tube to rotate smoothly on the supporting rope stay. At the bottom the weight of the sail and tubes presses down onto a flat plastic disc that is threaded onto the rope core like a bead. This is the main bearing and the bottom of the tube just slips around on the smooth disc. Other 'spacer' bearings are placed inside the tubes to keep the luff-stay rope central. Putting the middle bearings inside the tube is a simple task involving pushing them into place with a stick already marked with the correct length of their location (by comparing it with the outside of the tube).

Planning.
The greatest challenge in this assembly is the forward planning.
For example when making up the top tube:
The rope has already passed correctly through the lower tube.
Thread on two top spacer bearings.
Mark the position of the central bearing on both tube and stick.
Pass the rope through the tube (then tie a temporary knot so as not to lose it). Push spacer up into place, drill, countersink and screw (care not to split wood).
Bottom bearing into place and fixed.
Untie top knot, thread on top bearing and fix. Add webbing strap.
Tie top bowline for halliard attachment allowing sufficient length to allow for assembly and disassembly of joint. Check this.
The sail will have to slide onto the roller from this end, which may mean untying the knot and removing the webbing tension strap, depending on the size of the luff sleeve. Do NOT lose the end of the rope into the tube.

Sail.

It will be seen that the sail luff length cannot be the total length available from bowsprit tip to the masthead turning block. The attachment of the halliard to the roller stay and the spare length needed for pulling the tubes apart can involve 100mm. The sail needs another 150mm to stretch tight. At the bottom, at least 150mm is taken up with the roller, the bearing, the shackle and length to get the drum angle correct for leading the roller line. The bowsprit will bend upwards under load despite the bobstay. It will also bend from side to side.

I worked out what shape I thought my sail ought to be and I made it myself by following instructions from two books. The first was my ancient, but treasured copy (cost one guinea) of 'Make your own sails' by Bowker and Budd (Macmillan) which although it dates from the 1950/60s gives sound advice. I double-checked it against 'Sails' (Adlard Coles) by Derek Harvey (*Also DCA, he is crewing my dinghy, page 19.*) dating from 1997 that confirmed the instructions. I doubt whether many people would take DIY dinghy cruising to this level, but I reasoned that it was a very small sail made from very thin cloth that my domestic sewing machine could handle, so if I didn't dare to tackle the job I would never get a better opportunity. There was a great deal more difficulty in sewing up my tent. It's not the most beautifully made sail, but it does the job and I learned a lot in making it. The sail area came to 29.4 sq. ft.

Everything can be rigged from inside the boat, though it does take some time. Assembling it is considerably quicker when it is rigged ashore. Whilst the many pieces may give an impression of complexity, each one was relatively simple to make using easily acquired materials and standard tools. When all the parts of the 'jigsaw' come together they produce a very useful system at minimal cost, which is an important goal for many DIY dinghy cruisers. When I began planning this system I did not want to add a sail that was capable of putting me in danger of being overwhelmed by a sudden gust of wind. I thought that I would construct it quite 'lightweight' so that some part of it would fail before I found myself in difficulties. I have been amazed at how durable it has been. I have operated it in winds stronger than I originally imagined and after several years of service I am still waiting for the 'weak link' to fail, whatever/wherever it is? It has transformed the off wind performance and has allowed me to cheat the tide to return home in the dying evening breeze on several occasions.

Sail area / Performance.

The sail I use in any given circumstances would depend on my location. I have to recognise that my boat has safe limits and it would not be my normal intention to sail in winds above force 4 in the open sea and probably force 5 in sheltered water. I also know that the sea breeze effect can sometimes lift onshore winds to these levels during summer afternoons and I would have to be prepared for this.

My approximate intended use of my sails is as follows.

Force 1 – 2	Main + Genoa	= 91sq ft.	(Off the wind)
Force 2 - 3/4	Main + Jib	= 80sq ft	
Force 4 / 5	Reefed Main + Jib	= 54sq ft	
Force 5 / 6	Storm Main + Jib	= 36sq ft	
Force 7 / 8	Storm Main or Jib	= 18sq ft	
F8	Sea anchor if possible.		

Bailing.

Most 'club' dinghies have only a hand bailer (simply made by reshaping a plastic milk container) and a sponge to remove bilge water. In the event of a capsize, nothing less than a bucket will have an effect on the water level inside most dinghies. It must be used vigorously ('a bucket in the hands of a frightened person,' is the usual phrase), which is exhausting. Most racing dinghies without raised floors or 'foot well' cockpits now rely on safety boats and the large, powered pumps that these craft usually carry.

A cruising dinghy must operate independently and usually carries its own pump that is, within reason, the bigger the better. Small dinghy pumps (with cycle pump actions) are usually inadequate and proper diaphragm pumps are strongly advised. These are not usually seen in small boats and it does take a mental adjustment for the novice to begin to accept that the installation of such a device requires some serious thought.

As soon as I started beating to windward in waves, single-handed in my dinghy, I quickly realised the need for proper equipment. Waves slap the side of the boat and a little water is splashed aboard. This is all right to begin with, but as the water begins to accumulate it becomes apparent that its weight might begin to counterbalance your own efforts. Do not underestimate this. A quantity of moving bilge water CAN capsize you, especially if you are caught-aback whilst tacking. Sooner or later you have to stop to remove the water and this may not be convenient. There is a need for a system that will allow you to use only one hand for pumping whilst the other one steers and it should be available for **both tacks** as the bilge water is always on the opposite side of the boat from you. Securing the drainage pipe outlet also needs some thought. On the more committed cruising Wayfarers I have seen big pumps and dual systems using permanently plumbed-in pipework, so that the water can be cleared from the leeward bilge with both crew sitting to windward. Such a system is expensive and can be heavy especially when the big-section, reinforced pipes are

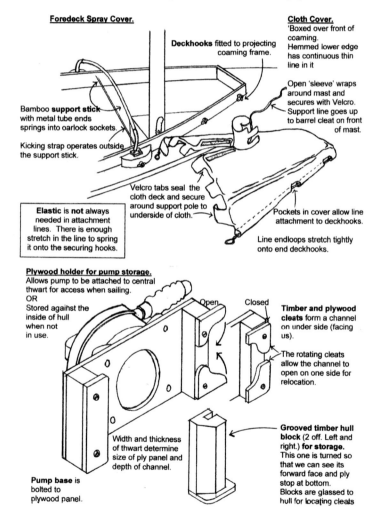

Foredeck Spray Cover.

Deckhooks fitted to projecting coaming frame.

Cloth Cover.
'Boxed over front of coaming.
Hemmed lower edge has continuous thin line in it

Open 'sleeve' wraps around mast and secures with Velcro. Support line goes up to barrel cleat on front of mast.

Bamboo **support stick** with metal tube ends springs into oarlock sockets.

Kicking strap operates outside the support stick.

Velcro tabs seal the cloth deck and secure around support pole to underside of cloth.

Elastic is **not** always needed in attachment lines. There is enough stretch in the line to spring it onto the securing hooks.

Pockets in cover allow line attachment to deckhooks.

Line endloops stretch tightly onto end deckhooks.

Plywood holder for pump storage.
Allows pump to be attached to central thwart for access when sailing.
OR
Stored against the inside of hull when not in use.

Open   Closed

Timber and plywood cleats form a channel on under side (facing us).

The rotating cleats allow the channel to open on one side for relocation.

Width and thickness of thwart determine size of ply panel and depth of channel.

Pump base is bolted to plywood panel.

Grooved timber hull block (2 off. Left and right.) **for storage.**
This one is turned so that we can see its forward face and ply stop at bottom. Blocks are glassed to hull for locating cleats

filled with water. Holes will have to be cut through the hull and skin fittings used. The neater ones have stern exit pipes, but this significantly increases the length and weight of filled pipes even though they are low in the boat

My solution has two strands.

    a)   Try to keep the water out by rigging a spray deflecting foredeck. and cockpit cover.

    b)   Use a mobile pumping system that can be transferred from one side of the craft to the other.

Foredeck spray deflector.

There are some older, class dinghies that have no foredeck that are used for cruising. Personally I would not regard this as safe, especially at sea, but I know that extended offshore journeys have been made in such craft. The DCA has a list of boat safety recommendations (outlined later), one of which states 'The vessel should at least have a foredeck.'

My Torch dinghy is unusual in not having a large permanent foredeck right back to the mast. The advantage of this is that I have extra accommodation space, but the disadvantage is that excessive spray can come aboard when beating against waves, unless I rig a deflector. It has the benefit of keeping the whole forward area above the buoyancy tank quite dry for equipment stowage.

My deflector (construction notes also included in 'Covers') is made from tent-type material secured to hooks around the front end of the boat's raised coaming, rather like the spraydeck on a canoe. It wraps around the mast and is secured with Velcro. The after end wraps over a temporary, bamboo-cane support bar and is fixed with more Velcro. It allows for normal kicking strap movement. The structure is simple and lightweight, but under certain conditions I do see it shedding lots of water (which would need to be pumped out) and keeping the forward area of the boat (and much kit) dry.

Diaphragm pump.

My pump is secured to a piece of plywood (see diagram) large enough to reach across the thwart from front to back. This board hooks onto the thwart at the front edge and it has two turn buttons to locate the rear edge onto the thwart. The hooking system is loose enough to allow the pump to slide to-and-fro a little, along the thwart. Locating the outer ends of the pipes is important, for you do not have a spare hand to hold them. My outlet pipe just neatly jams into the shroud-securing loop on deck, pointing outboard. The intake pipe must be jammed into the gap between floorboards above the place where the bilge water collects. It is worth making fixing points if they do not naturally occur.

Stopping the boat.

Anchoring.

Small sailing dinghies don't usually have anchors. They may not have a bow fairlead or a suitably strong fixing cleat at the bow unless they are kept afloat on a mooring (which means they are 'bigger' dinghies). Generally, owners can sail for years without needing to anchor because usually they operate from the shore to the shore. The first actual anchoring that many sailors will do probably comes as part of working towards some kind of sailing proficiency certificate that will require them to anchor. They may do it only a couple of times, in a borrowed boat, to satisfy the requirement. The anchor may be just a folding grapnel on a line, in a bucket, put aboard for one sailing session to enable the exercise.

If this should describe your anchoring experience then I would recommend actively extending it, because as a dinghy cruiser, you may well have to stay overnight riding to an anchor and there is a great deal to learn if you want to rest easily. For peace of mind you must have a proper anchor with proper chain on a secure rope rode, which comes aboard through a chunky fairlead and is strongly attached to the boat. The anchor is one place to legitimately have weight in a dinghy, but don't overdo the chain. Four or five metres of the right quality should be sufficient for most circumstances. (DCA recommends 3 – 4 metres, see Safety Ch 5.) An informative anchoring article by Steve Bradwell, 'Making an anchor weight.' 217/51 might prove useful for the larger-craft sailor.

Due to the total weight of the anchor and chain I decided to modify my floorboards to get this weight central and as low as possible in the boat. The anchor warp is the problem. The most common solution involves using a bucket to hold it. I made up a rotating reel that I secured beneath my floorboards. It stops the rope from getting kinked and tangled but it is a bit fiddly to re-roll the warp. I don't mind too much, because I am not a frequent user of the anchor, preferring moorings if I can find them. I have seen really major arrangements on Wayfarers involving reels with winding handles and very long warps, but that's for the real sea goers.

Some useful tips.

Any arrangement MUST allow for the securing of the bitter end of the anchor warp on the boat. If it is in a bucket this may involve it exiting through a hole in the bottom of the bucket (then it may not bail well). If it is on a reel it could be attached to a swivel but it must have a solidly secured axle arrangement.

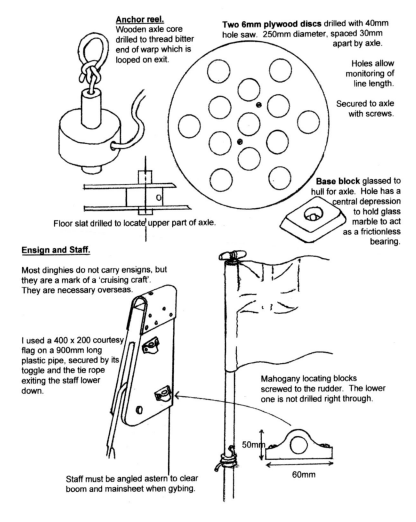

Anchor reel.
Wooden axle core drilled to thread bitter end of warp which is looped on exit.

Two 6mm plywood discs drilled with 40mm hole saw. 250mm diameter, spaced 30mm apart by axle.

Holes allow monitoring of line length.

Secured to axle with screws.

Floor slat drilled to locate upper part of axle.

Base block glassed to hull for axle. Hole has a central depression to hold glass marble to act as a frictionless bearing.

Ensign and Staff.

Most dinghies do not carry ensigns, but they are a mark of a 'cruising craft'. They are necessary overseas.

I used a 400 x 200 courtesy flag on a 900mm long plastic pipe, secured by its toggle and the tie rope exiting the staff lower down.

Mahogany locating blocks screwed to the rudder. The lower one is not drilled right through.

50mm

60mm

Staff must be angled astern to clear boom and mainsheet when gybing.

- I use 6mm braided polyester line. This has a minimum breaking load of about 700kgs, which is plenty (even when considering snatch loads and tying knots), for my purpose. I have a piece of cloth to wrap around it where it passes into the fairlead. I usually cruise in rivers and estuaries, which are shallow, so my 25 metres of warp have rarely been deployed more than half way. See the dimensioned diagram of my reel that perfectly holds the 25 metres of line. (DCA recommends 30 metres of 8mm.)

- Keep the anchor accessible in the boat. It may have to be used in an emergency if there is some kind of serious gear failure.
- Anchors, chain and shackles go rusty which can make a mess in the bottom of boats; stain sails etc. so keep up to the maintenance of washing them off prior to the winter and dabbing galvanising paint on affected areas.
- Don't use folding grapnels on string. They rotate like propellers when being dropped in a tidal flow (so they MUST have a greased swivel). Their effectiveness can be tested whilst ashore by digging them into a beach and pulling along the rope. You won't use them again!
- Learn some strategies for dealing with a fouled anchor **before** you get it caught. At least have a plastic bottle with a handle on it and a line, to buoy or trip with. It will give you the option of leaving the anchor to get further equipment or assistance.
- If you are going to spend most of your time on inland waters/navigable rivers you may find that rond anchors, dog anchors (See Duncan Gilchrist 192/47), or even tent pegs are preferred.

Beaching.

A very informative DCA article by Alan Glanville in Bull. 162/30-31 covers his different techniques for anchoring in different tidal circumstances. Read it. It is excellent.

Staying on the shore overnight is a popular strategy with dinghy cruisers. It allows for a change of scene and activity. One can walk and explore, meet other people, top up supplies, go for drinks and meals and it makes different toilet arrangements possible. It works best with High Water in the morning/evening in tidal situations. This means that the boat will be out of the water most of the night as the tide ebbs and then returns. It is essential that the quality of the bottom and its levelness have been checked before allowing the boat to settle down. There are plenty of horror stories about sharp stakes, boulders and precipitous drops to be read (John Deacon 029/10). Creeks and saltings are possible stopping places almost uniquely accessible for dinghies to go aground. They are wonderful for solitude, bird/wildlife watching and stargazing.

Being aware of wind direction and tidal movement is essential at all times when ashore, especially when making temporary stops at beaches for lunch. Most loaded cruising dinghies are too heavy for their crews to get back into the water once they are aground and consequently it is advisable to keep a sharp eye on them or treat them as if they were ballasted boats.

Ballasted boats.
How can having a ballasted boat be different? A boat is a boat isn't it? Well it is a bit more complicated than that. This is a continuation of the earlier discussion about open dinghies and dinghies-with-lids.

When you sails in an open dinghy you can be casual about going aground. If the boat touches the bottom the crew can give a hefty shove with an oar or if the bottom is firm enough, step out and push off to get afloat again. With a ballasted boat you have to be more wary. Being grounded on a muddy bottom on a falling tide is a recipe for a long tedious wait until the tide returns to re-float the

Small ballasted boats are handled the same as much bigger craft.

boat. Doing this at high water, when the tides are moving towards neaps, is a well-known, nightmare scenario. Ballast on boats usually means they have a deeper draught and therefore the hull grounds earlier and in deeper water than the open dinghy. If they

91

do not have a deep draught the chances of getting stuck are probably increased. In a tidal situation, the shallower the water the boat grounds in, the less time there is available to float it again.

Fin keel yachts can be released by heeling them over; bilge keels are trickier and the stub keels found on ballasted dinghies, even worse. The open dinghy usually has a centreboard, so there is a warning as it touches the bottom in water still deep enough for the boat to be turned and sailed away, providing the helm knows what they are doing (hold it, don't lift the board too soon).

A ballasted boat aground stands a chance of floating again if a crewmember can be moved quickly into the tender. If this fails the skipper may want to lay an anchor out towards the deeper water. On a soft bottom this will require a tender. A tender might also be needed for freeing a fouled anchor and so there is a strong incentive for tender towing. They are 'insurance' and an essential sailing tool for certain sailing circumstances with ballasted boats. Also see, Singlehanded anchoring 216/56 Doug Heslop.

Knowing about these circumstances subconsciously affects the way that boats are sailed. Ballasted boats stick more closely to the channel and do not take risks when approaching the shore. If the tide is ebbing at a lunchtime stopover the skipper needs to know the depth and to constantly monitor it, to avoid getting caught out. On several rallies that I have attended, sailors of boats the same size or not much bigger than mine, have towed tenders. This is the tell tale mark of a different mind-set between the two types of craft. I would never consider dragging another boat around behind my dinghy. If I want to go ashore I just sail up to it and step out. With a ballasted boat the easy way is to treat the craft as a yacht. To go ashore, one drops the anchor and crosses in the tender, even for lunch. The same applies to overnight stops and often, to visiting another craft afloat. I would just sail up alongside, as the lightness of my boat does not pose a threat of damage between the two craft. Of course, all these manoeuvres are possible in ballasted boats, it is just that gradually the skipper comes to operate in the safest manner and will begin to exercise caution and do things the 'right way' using methods that reduce risk for all ballasted boats, including bigger yachts. This is one reason why I have stayed on the 'open dinghy' side of the divide. My own feeling is that if I want to sail 'as a yacht', then I would probably move to one in the 18 – 25 ft size range which would give me more space and comfort. There is a group called the Trail-Sail Association specifically for this size and type of craft (more details under 'Contacts'). I do not want to have to sail in this way in a 13/14ft boat and give up my ability to carelessly sail the river's shallow edges or run ashore for lunch with hardly a thought. I also want to move with oars and not to use a motor, which can be another mark of the divide.

I have to stress that these are my preferences, at my age, at this time. I do not do cross-Channel sails in my dinghy. If I did I would probably want ballast. There are many reasons why I will have to change as life progresses. I expect to eventually move into a marina instead of dragging my boat and trolley over the river wall; begin to use an outboard instead of oars and want the comfort of a 'lid' over me as I make a brew or go to sleep. (See 'In Praise of Lids' Jones. Bull. 193/50 describing how a 'lid' can extend the sailing season.) In the meantime I appreciate the qualities of freedom that the open, lightweight dinghy offers.

Fender/rollers.
Having boat rollers or yacht fenders may allow a grounded boat to be returned to the water 201/27, 29, 37. I use fenders and it is reassuring for me to know that I can always get my boat back to the water. The main effect of fender/rollers is to break the suction of the wet beach/mud against the bottom of the boat (see later story). In extreme circumstances boats can be pulled up firm beaches using rollers with the mainsheet attached to the anchor and extending warp. It takes time and organisation. When the boat is aground it can be uncomfortable living aboard if it is not level. Beaches almost always slope. Dinghies are often secured facing along the beach rather than up and down it, to minimise the sloping effect. On a hard beach the boat may tip from side to side as you move across inside it, so a small amount of digging (using a trowel) may be required to remove sand from below the upper bilge and transfer it to the lower one. An alternative is to secure the boat roller/fender under the lower bilge (see centre pages), always ensuring that it does not float away when the water returns.

Fenders become essential when stopping in marinas, in locks, against quays, pontoons or other craft. Most dinghies do not have sufficient cleats for breast ropes and springs, as used on yachts, but I found that they are rarely necessary. I usually use the tent securing line just below my gunwale to fasten to and my boat is small enough to tuck into sheltered, quiet corners. It will be accepted alongside other larger craft which act as fenders against walls and piers especially in harbours with a big tidal range. A variety of warps will be needed for all circumstances.

Marina Mooring.

A method we employ now to secure the boat alongside, is to have two slightly diagonal ropes, one forward, one backwards, <u>for the bow fixing</u>, a triangular tie (lower diagram). They are not tight and allow the boat some movement slightly ahead and astern. Being diagonal they triangulate and act like short springs in restricting the range of this movement. The back of the boat has a looser line attached just astern of the beam, running up onto the pontoon behind the boat, like a spring. Its length allows the boat's stern to drift 45 degrees out, away from the pontoon, with the triangulated bow-fixing lines controlling the back and forward movement. The boat's rear is free to rotate around its bow. A wind shift onto the opposite side of the boat floats it back to lie with its fenders alongside the pontoon, because we secure facing as much towards the wind as possible, with the wind favouring the side nearest the pontoon. Generally the boat just moves slowly 10-15 degrees back and forth responding to stray wind

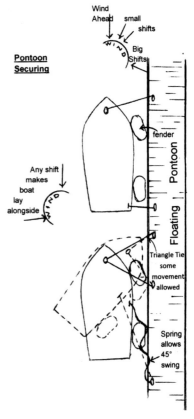

shifts that penetrate into the sheltered marina locations that we always chose with great care. This movement is imperceptible inside the tent. (See Tent Testing later.)

To get in or out of the boat, we reach for the stern spring and use it to pull the boat back in alongside to step in or out. We have found that there is an added advantage when securing to floating pontoons in this way. If we are tightly fastened alongside (top boat diagram), when other users walk along the pontoon their footfall is transmitted to our boat through ropes and fenders, but with the boat freed, this vibration no longer affects us and we have a quieter time.

Dave Jennings prepares his tent.
Look at the amount of kit.

Cliff Martin's afternoon snooze.

DCA boats gather for an annual rally at Holy Island.

Chris Waite's 'Tit Willow' deep cockpit hull

'Polly Wee' deep dinghy

(Below) Howard Rice aboard Scamp.

Scamp under sail.

'Jady Lane' with sunshade
This boat has sailed
Cross-Channel

Cliff Martin surfs his Mirror
Probably the smallest
practical dinghy cruiser.

Alan Glanville's homebuilt
Ness yawl 'Lowly Worm'.
Pic. Ed Wingfield.

Torch '*Tyne*' sailing with son Martin.

Note bowsprit, roller headsail, and line below gunwhale for tent attachment.
Ply transom pad for outboard.
Short distance from gaff jaws to boom that limits reefing distance and badly creased (inefficient) sail!

Black tent absorbs heat.
No need for windows to be square.
Secured fender chocks boat level on sloping beach.
Reflecting strips on extremities including projecting boom/gaff.
Doors roll up and secure with Velcro tabs.

Hooped tents at Beale Park.
River Thames boat show.

Wish you were here?

John Hughes' Family Cat 'Star Chaser'.   Shallow draft, big tent, stands level

Keith Muscott's Mirror 16 'Footloose' at   Chris Heike's Wanderer 'Herbie', Holy Island
Poll Domhain. Access to 'secret' locations.   Thanks to Ed Wingfield & Tim Roberts

Moorings.
As I frequently sail in popular tidal rivers that have many moorings I usually prefer to overnight on them rather than anchor if I can. Moorings mean the boat moves about less than on an anchor, there is no chance of snagging my anchor underwater and I do not have to show a riding light or day signal unless I choose to. I seek as much shelter as I can find, preferably towards the edge, and look for an unused (dirty) mooring. I check its condition as much as possible and the water depth compared with the tidal range. Plunging a firmly held oar down into the water will give an indication. Yacht moorings may have big eye-spliced, fixed warps, often too thick to pass through a dinghy fairlead so I have my own stout rope for 'mooring to a mooring' that I pass through my fairlead and then secure to my mast. Using my rope keeps my boat clean as I don't have to bring the dirty warp (and its attendant wildlife) aboard. Releasing it is a simple task.

Shelter.
So far in this book, I have taken my ordinary little boat and checked that it will work for cruising, which imposes a different set of demands from the usual dinghy sailing. Any modifications that I have suggested for rudder, tiller, centerboard, anchor and sails etc. should also make my boat safer and more reliable for normal sailing. Having decided that I have a viable craft I must begin to look at what additional things I need specially for cruising and the most important new piece of equipment is probably the tent.

The Tent.
There is no proven 'best tent' that everyone accepts as being the ultimate design. In fact there are as many ways to make the tent, as there are people and boats engaged in dinghy cruising. On this subject the options are infinite and that's what makes it so interesting. To be as helpful as I can I'll make some observations about what I learned and the choices that I made, but remember there are easier, quicker tents than mine. In doing this I can only scratch the surface of this vast topic.

The Specification.
When we make anything we usually begin by thinking of its function, what it has to do. With tents this is where we immediately diverge from each other, because the functions throw up conflicting requirements and some people will choose one option whilst others

may go by a different route. One of my decisions was to have as large a tent as practicable to give myself the comfort of internal space, but this increases windage, uses more cloth, costs more and increases the stress on the support structure. A bigger tent may take longer to erect, be heavier and take up more space when folded. This is typical of the problems brought to light when considering only a single aspect of this complex topic. I read what Margaret Dye had to say in her excellent book on dinghy cruising and accepted what she said about the lack of headroom if one just throws a sheet over the boom and fastens it to the gunwales. However, I have seen many boats using this system and I would suggest that it is probably still the most popular method used. It has the great virtues of being simple and quick. She uses it herself on occasions (as she explains) and illustrates it on the covers (1997 version) of her book.

Decisions. Decisions.

When I started on my tent I had many questions rushing around my head. They went along these lines.

Should it go over the boom? If not, why not?

If not. How is it supported along the ridge?

What is the order of importance of these factors?

Watertight   Rot resistant   Cost

Strength   Availability   Weight

Wind Noise   Colour   Insulation

What system is used to secure it to the boat?

Does it form a draught proof seal at the gunwale? If so, how?

Should there be windows? Where? How many? How big?

How long does it take to erect a tent?

Can it be done singlehanded? From inside the boat only?

How is it supported? (At Mast. Shrouds. Transom.)

Will it leak at the mast?

Where are the doors? How many?

Do the sides roll up? How are they secured?

How long does it take to dismantle?

Where does it stow, how much space does it take?

Can the boat be sailed/moved with the tent up? Is this necessary?

Is there access to the anchor/warp/bow fairlead with tent erected?

Is the external shape important for wind resistance?

Is ventilation a design consideration? Is condensation a problem?

How well does it have to be made?

Fabrication.

I am lucky that I live close to the water and when I heard that a group of camping dinghies was stopping nearby, I went along to photograph them and I was greatly encouraged at seeing that they all used completely different tent systems. None of them was sophisticated or high tech and the standard of construction was average DIY. They were just enjoying themselves and the tents were made up from odds and ends they had managed to pull together, using whatever materials they had available, canvas, bits of plywood, sticks, it didn't matter. It was OK to be amateur and that was nice to know. I went back to the dinghy park and started work on planning my tent.

First I sat in the boat on the thwart and 'measured' the height of my head with my hand, across onto the mast. That was my 'sitting headroom'. If I could secure the boom and gaff at that height at the mast and a similar or slightly lower level at the transom it would define the ridge of the tent. If I took a line from the same point on the mast down to the bow of the boat that could be the line of my bow cuddy and I would have the whole shape determined.

As I went along I attempted to answer all my questions for myself, and this is what I decided, but it may not be right for other people in other craft. My tent goes over the boom. The main argument against this is based on the fact that the (wet) sail will be rubbing on your head inside the tent unless you remove it from the spars, which takes time and gives you a storage problem. I got around this by making a reasonably snug 'sausage' cover with a full-length zip, to catch the boom, sail and gaff in. Incidentally I found that this cover was invaluable for protecting the sail in general use and especially when moving the gear around outside the boat whilst preparing for trailing.

'Modern-materials' canopy cloths that are watertight, rot resistant and specified for their weights and strengths can be obtained from specialist suppliers (see 'Suppliers'). I obtained catalogues, compared prices and specifications of cloths and fastenings and purchased materials from a couple of companies. I used Polyurethane coated nylon 150 gms/sq.m. for all covers/bags etc. Whilst this would also have sufficed for a normal tent I decided that I wanted a heavier fabric that might be easier to control in heavy weather. I used a waterproof nylon 255/265-gms/sq.m. that was described as being extremely tough and long lasting. I used black coloured cloth for my tent in an effort to collect and retain as much heat as possible (especially first thing in the morning), to make it dark for sleeping and to give me the impression of being in

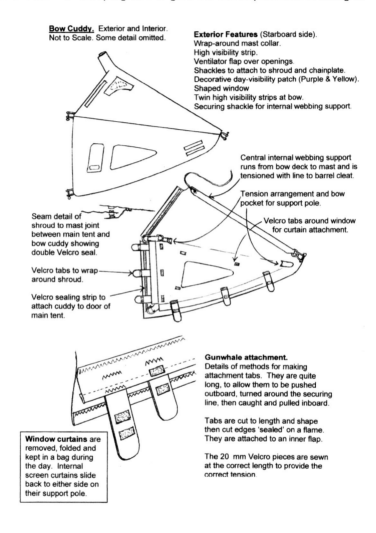

Bow Cuddy. Exterior and Interior.
Not to Scale. Some detail omitted.

Exterior Features (Starboard side).
Wrap-around mast collar.
High visibility strip.
Ventilator flap over openings.
Shackles to attach to shroud and chainplate.
Decorative day-visibility patch (Purple & Yellow).
Shaped window
Twin high visibility strips at bow.
Securing shackle for internal webbing support.

Central internal webbing support
runs from bow deck to mast and is
tensioned with line to barrel cleat.

Tension arrangement and bow
pocket for support pole.

Velcro tabs around window
for curtain attachment.

Seam detail of
shroud to mast joint
between main tent and
bow cuddy showing
double Velcro seal.

Velcro tabs to wrap
around shroud.

Velcro sealing strip to
attach cuddy to door of
main tent.

Gunwhale attachment.
Details of methods for making
attachment tabs. They are quite
long, to allow them to be pushed
outboard, turned around the securing
line, then caught and pulled inboard.

Tabs are cut to length and shape
then cut edges 'sealed' on a flame.
They are attached to an inner flap.

The 20 mm Velcro pieces are sewn
at the correct length to provide the
correct tension.

Window curtains are
removed, folded and
kept in a bag during
the day. Internal
screen curtains slide
back to either side on
their support pole.

a 'solid' cabin. This is not a popular choice with most cruisers who seem to prefer the lighter colours, beige and cream, to give them a light and airy feel. I believe that green and blue are not always 'actively' selected because they tend to make the occupants inside look ill, but, as these are the most usual colours for canvas and cheap woven polypropylene sheets, they are widely used.

Needless to say, my choices were not cheap. By the time I had finished I spent more on the tent than I did on buying the boat.
Together with the cloth I purchased:
PVC window material .5mm thick, Mosquito netting for ventilators.
Velcro. Polyester Webbing reinforcing tape.
Threads for the different colours.
Zips and sliders. Turn-button fabric fasteners. Alloy D rings.
Reflective tape, to make my black tent visible to lights at night.

The Bow Cuddy.
I made my tent in two sections. I had a bow cuddy from just inside the tip of the bow up to the mast, across to the shrouds and then down to the chain plate. The general arrangement is shown in the diagram. This can be erected fairly swiftly and gives an immediate degree of shelter. Many dinghy cruisers, particularly on the bigger craft do not include the foredeck area inside their tent. I include it with mine because my unusual foredeck that does not reach as far back as the mast gives me valuable living-accommodation space forward of the mast and under the deck. When living aboard, the top of my short foredeck is a good place to store the jib, my oilies, lifejacket and boots to keep them out of the way. This cuddy can be erected as a temporary shelter when stopping for midday meals and even toilet breaks if necessary.

The main tent canopy.
The main body of the tent attaches to the cuddy with Velcro tape; is secured to the mast with ties and supported along its ridge by the boom. The boom in its turn is supported by a scissor type boom-crutch at the transom. I have an 'eaves pole' structure to give larger internal space. Many boats use their oars for this, but I decided not to do so, because I wanted to keep them available for use in moving the boat whilst the tent was erected if that should become necessary. Both tent and cuddy are secured along the gunwale using a method described by Margaret Dye in 'Dinghy Cruising' which uses barrel cleats and a line, instead of hooks, which could snag on things. One of the neatest systems that I have seen subsequently was on John Perry's boat. His drawings for a 'slotted gunwale system' DCA Bull. 109/11 is reproduced here. Webbing tabs on my tent pass around the line below the gunwale and secure back to themselves with Velcro. I chose a spacing of about .5m to coincide with the cleats on the hull but it could be a bit further than this. I used standard 50mm wide tape that would have been strong

enough at half that width, but it spreads the load along the line. I attached the tape to an inner flap on the tent rather than the edge of the cloth in order to further spread the load on the cloth and to give a longer overlapping flap of tent cloth at the gunwale to shed rainwater and reduce the chances of wave splash entering the boat. The freeboard is quite small in places and with rough

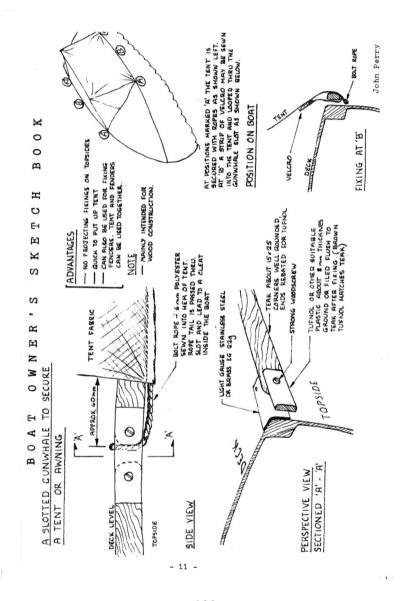

conditions I guess it would allow water to come in. When I am inside the tent the small side deck is a tempting shelf on which to put small objects (toothbrush, small torch) for there is no visible gap, but I have to remember that it will still be possible for them to slide overboard under the flap, if I am not careful.

The flaps at the back of the tent are held together with turn-button fabric fasteners. This allows the flaps to be opened in hot weather to get a good airflow through the tent. Having a stern opening allows access to the rudder, the ensign, and securing or mooring lines when in port.

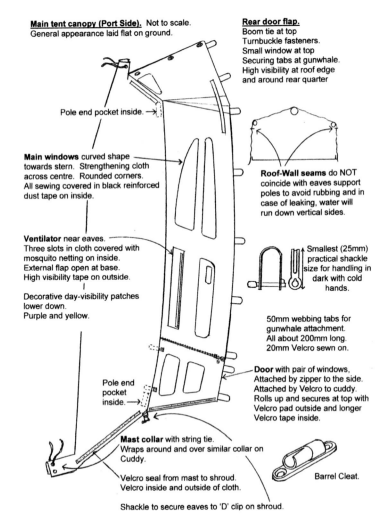

Main tent canopy (Port Side). Not to scale. General appearance laid flat on ground.

Pole end pocket inside. →

Main windows curved shape towards stern. Strengthening cloth across centre. Rounded corners. All sewing covered in black reinforced dust tape on inside.

Ventilator near eaves. Three slots in cloth covered with mosquito netting on inside. External flap open at base. High visibility tape on outside.

Decorative day-visibility patches lower down. Purple and yellow.

Pole end pocket inside. →

Mast collar with string tie. Wraps around and over similar collar on Cuddy.

Velcro seal from mast to shroud. Velcro inside and outside of cloth.

Shackle to secure eaves to 'D' clip on shroud.

Rear door flap.
Boom tie at top
Turnbuckle fasteners.
Small window at top
Securing tabs at gunwhale.
High visibility at roof edge and around rear quarter

Roof-Wall seams do NOT coincide with eaves support poles to avoid rubbing and in case of leaking, water will run down vertical sides.

Smallest (25mm) practical shackle size for handling in dark with cold hands.

50mm webbing tabs for gunwhale attachment. All about 200mm long. 20mm Velcro sewn on.

Door with pair of windows, Attached by zipper to the side. Attached by Velcro to cuddy. Rolls up and secures at top with Velcro pad outside and longer Velcro tape inside.

Barrel Cleat.

There is a door on either side just astern of the shrouds. As the tent has to attach to the cuddy it is a simple matter to use this joint as the forward edge of the door. The other (rear) edge of the door is formed by a vertical zip about 500 - 750mm further back. Having a door on either side is important in marinas where the boat can lay on either side of a pontoon. It is worth noting that my boat has no real access across it under such circumstances (unless one clambers in at one door and out of the other) so I have to be the very last boat on any row and then I seal it off. Usually my boat is so small that I can squeeze into little corners inaccessible to other larger craft.

Windows don't have to be square, although this is the simplest shape to sew for the novice. All external features such as windows, doors, vents and reflective strips effectively draw shapes and lines on the outside of the tent, so I tried to harmonize them a little, to deflect the eye away from the wrinkled, 'black-boxiness' of my structure. I use loose (purple) curtain flaps secured by Velcro tabs on the corners inside my windows. Also inside I have two (yellow) curtains across the beam of the boat above the thwart where the brighter colour 'lightens' the interior. One or both curtains can be drawn in from either side to divide the sleeping area off from the front of the boat. The option of two 'rooms' is often convenient.

Condensation can be a problem with any tent structure in anything but the best weather. The tent has a great deal of natural ventilation but I added vents near the eaves in an effort to increase air movement higher up. The flatter the roof, the greater the chance of dripping inside, so this could be another plus point for the simple, over-the-boom tent which has steeply sloping sides to carry water down to the gunwales. Absorbent kitchen cloths are essential to wipe down the tent ceiling on damp or cold mornings. Having a black tent generates discernable warmth in the early morning and dries the tent as rapidly and as soon as possible.

Securing the tent to fixings and rigging is done mainly with shackles. The best ones have a captive pin of some sort. They can be wonderfully expensive. They fasten onto 'D' rings sewn to the cloth and are reinforced with 25mm woven black tape. I was successful in lashing 'D' rings to the shrouds to make a securing point for the eaves.

Tent poles.
The qualities needed in poles are lightness and stiffness at a reasonable price. If they float that would be an added bonus. After

Tent. Supporting Structure. (Some details omitted for clarity.)

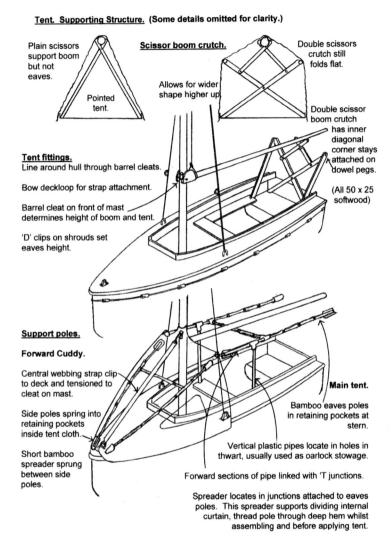

Plain scissors support boom but not eaves.

Pointed tent.

Scissor boom crutch.

Allows for wider shape higher up

Double scissors crutch still folds flat.

Double scissor boom crutch has inner diagonal corner stays attached on dowel pegs.

(All 50 x 25 softwood)

Tent fittings.
Line around hull through barrel cleats.

Bow deckloop for strap attachment.

Barrel cleat on front of mast determines height of boom and tent.

'D' clips on shrouds set eaves height.

Support poles.

Forward Cuddy.

Central webbing strap clip to deck and tensioned to cleat on mast.

Side poles spring into retaining pockets inside tent cloth.

Short bamboo spreader sprung between side poles.

Main tent.

Bamboo eaves poles in retaining pockets at stern.

Vertical plastic pipes locate in holes in thwart, usually used as oarlock stowage.

Forward sections of pipe linked with 'T junctions.

Spreader locates in junctions attached to eaves poles. This spreader supports dividing internal curtain, thread pole through deep hem whilst assembling and before applying tent.

examining a number of different plumbing tubes in DIY supermarkets I concluded that 22mm rigid white plastic overflow pipe was potentially useful as it comes with a variety of end fittings (link, 'T', and 'corner') that can be used to build it into various shapes. The fittings are not indestructible and are being used for a purpose for which they were not designed, so it is safest to carry a couple of spares as 'insurance'. They are all cheap and easy to obtain. Whilst it might not naturally float it can be made buoyant by fitting wooden plugs into the tube ends. Wooden plugs can be 'glued' to smooth plastic with silicone sealant as used for bonding uPVC window frames to brickwork. I found that for lengths up to about 1 metre the tube was fine, but over that length it became progressively more flexible.

For lengths up to 2 metres it is difficult to find anything stiffer and lighter than good old-fashioned bamboo poles. They are obtainable from garden centres but you have to shop around to find precisely what is required. Parallel-sided poles of a good length can be sold individually commanding high prices. Tapered poles may be packaged with six or ten together reasonably cheaply. I found that the bamboo poles could be made to fit into the water pipe end fittings (mentioned above) by simply bonding glassfibre tape around their ends when they were too thin. They can be further secured by attaching the plastic end fittings to them using polyester car body filler packed into the fittings and allowing it to set. This will produce a support frame combining bamboo and plastic pipe with standard sized connections throughout.

It is important to protect the bamboo with marine varnish to stop it from rotting when it is in prolonged contact with damp conditions. In order to make the finish adhere properly the hard shiny surface of the bamboo has to be lightly rubbed away with fine abrasive paper prior to applying the varnish. Poles that go to port and starboard may be identified with red or black plastic tape, but they should be interchangeable wherever possible because sooner or later, they will have to be used to erect the tent in the dark when colour is difficult to distinguish.

All of my poles fit into a custom-made bag that is secured with elastic ties just under the side decks towards the stern. My 'poles' bag resembles a long fishing rod bag with a shorter pocket for smaller poles on one side. When all the poles are inside, it could act as a small amount of additional buoyancy. I have another similar bag for the scissor-like boom crutch. Both of my tent canopies together with the curtains will fit into a bag about 1metre long and about 150mm diameter.

The making of the tent was no small undertaking and it cost about the same as a good suit of sails. It took many hours of fitting and sewing and it was not the kind of task to embark upon without being certain that I was committed to using it. Some dinghy cruisers start out with a golf umbrella (even quicker shelter than my cuddy) and a cheap polypropylene over-boom canopy cover from a builder's merchant. There is much to recommend this approach for anyone still experimenting with the sport. It takes me about an hour to put up or dismantle the whole tent structure and convert from sailing to living or visa versa. This is too long. It is worth trying to devise a more rapid system aiming for 15 to 20 minutes as a reasonable target. This probably indicates a 'pram hood' type system for a cuddy and the main tent to use hooped frames of some sort (see Colin Bell 194/43).

Colin Bell's hooped tent, probably quick to assemble.

Having said this, it is a comfortable feeling when it is up. It is pretty solid and spacious ... and yes, it does feel so much like home that I am always reluctant to start taking it all down again. However, it isn't always idyllic, as experience has shown. Here are a couple of scary stories bringing together a number of the elements from this chapter with some questions to answer at the end. Before you start the stories, remember, it isn't always like this.

Tent Testing.

We had arrived at the Danish island of Fur (pronounced 'Foor') and secured the boat. To this point it had been sunny, but clouds were building and rain was forecast, so we decided to put up our tent quickly. We had got it on just in time to hear rain speckling it and we scurried around inside fastening it down to the gunwale rope with its Velcro tabs, when, Bang! It suddenly went mad. Huge gusts of wind hit us with powerful blows from the side. We had secured with the bows facing the wind and the seawall, but an instant, mighty blast hit us like a brick wall against our starboard side where the boat was securely tied to the jetty/walkway with two tight breast ropes. It immediately ripped open all the Velcro tabs on the opposite, port side. The roof lifted up, sucked by the low pressure on the outside and the support poles became detached from each other, but still attached to the cloth. Beneath it, both Alison my wife and I were struggling to support the starboard side poles whilst holding the flogging tent down on the opposite side. The approaching whistling noise of the wind had been like a jet aircraft coming-in to land. It instantly turned into a continuous roar as the wind hit us. A huge downpour of rain and hail struck us with great force, yet we were well below the walkway, the jetty and protected by the harbour walls on two sides. The starboard poles were now bending amazingly just from the compression and the loose tent side was beating violently. I tried to unzip the doors to let the blast pass straight through, but it made little difference other than to soak us in a horizontal stream of fire-hose strength rainwater. We just hung onto as much as we could and waited for it to slowly subside.

It died briefly and we quickly reattached all the Velcro tabs and got the poles together just as it started up again, so we hung on some more, but it never quite had the intensity of that original strike. I had never experienced anything like it before. It lasted about 10 – 15 minutes at its worst, then fell to similar but lesser events, sometimes with the wind shifting to the opposite direction, and back again. We had a lot of sorting out to do afterwards. Maybe it was a 'microburst'? It was a frightening, amazing and exhausting time.

This freak natural event changed the way that we secured to pontoons in future (See Marina Mooring earlier). We had always secured at front and back with a couple of breast ropes, but now we felt that if the boat had been free to swing more head-to-wind in the biggest shift, it would have been better. The longer shape presented to the wind when pointing towards it made the tent cloth quieter and it didn't try to lift. The lift had been extreme when the long axis of the tent was secured across the wind, presenting quite a short cross-section shape that could generate a mighty vacuum on its top and lee side, sufficient to open up all our 50mm wide Velcro fasteners set at 500 mm centres. I would not have thought this possible and probably it will never happen again, but in sailing, according to Murphy's Law, 'If it can, it will'.

Do you wear your lifejacket in bed?

In late afternoon and failing wind I chose to anchor overnight in the middle of a wide, shallow side-bay, off the main estuary so that the boat would be able to comfortably rotate right around its anchor, automatically positioning itself to wind and tide direction. The tide in here hardly had a direction, it simply rose and fell. I would take the soft ground in the middle of the night, for a couple of hours on either side of low water for some steady rest. During the evening it fell to a mirror calm and other boats that had gently sailed in the main bay were obliged to chug slowly home to the top of the estuary whilst still enjoying the wonderful sunshine well into the late evening. I shared it too and didn't go to bed until about 10.45 when a faint air just dimpled the water.

From being deeply asleep in the darkness I was dreaming of waking up to a turbulent rocking, then I became aware of the noise of a violent wind. It was as if the sound was in a tunnel, remote and distant, but coming closer, rushing towards me. Suddenly, with a roar, it was here and I was in it. I was awake and opening my eyes to look around me at my tent cloth flexing and straining. The support poles were buckling under the shock of powerful gusts. I couldn't believe it. What was happening? Was this real weather? Was I awake? All forecasts had said that there would be no wind, but they were wrong, very wrong. It was at least force 5 and the boat was twisting and turning in the gusts. This was serious. I lay trying to comprehend, flattening myself onto my bed and clutching my sleeping bag tightly around my neck. Where had this come from? I looked at my watch to see how long it would be before I found security by descending onto the mud and I was amazed to see that it was only 11.45. I had only been asleep for an hour. This was crazy.

I was immediately conscious of being on a small anchor that I had never tried before, on a light warp. My dinghy is small and I had been looking to save some of the excessive weight of my previous ground tackle, so I'd changed it. The wind was straight from the head of the bay. If my anchor dragged or the line failed I would go directly down the bay and out into the open sea. It was a frightening thought. It would happen quickly. I didn't want to think about it. What could I do? There was an overpowering desire to just lay still, clinging to warmth, hoping that it would all go away, subside, sort itself out, but it wasn't going to.

The boat was bucking as the waves gathered force due to quite a long clear fetch. If something broke my only option was to try to row, but I was lightly clothed and in bed, the tent was up and the oars were tucked away in the bilge. It would take me ages before I even got an oar in the water. The tent windage would sail me away very rapidly. What if the worst happened? I might go broadside in the bigger waves at sea with the chance of a capsize. Can you swim in a sleeping bag? I was scared. Imagine getting out of the bag inside the collapsed tent with the boat upside down on top of it and all the loose gear being hurled around as if it was in a washing machine, in freezing water, in the dark. It was no good lying in bed hoping that it wouldn't happen. I must start from now as if it HAD just happened. Even getting out of the bag might improve my chances.

It was cold when I got out, but I scrambled forward. The first thing that I did was to take the anchor warp from where it was secured to the wooden foredeck cleat and extend it to tie it around the base of the mast. The warp wasn't parcelled where it went through the bow fairlead and it was tricky to reach from inside the tent with bits of gear in the way. I wrapped my sunhat (as the first thing that came to hand) around the warp to do the best job possible and jammed it in the fairlead. Getting hold of the line I was encouraged that it wasn't bar-tight. Although it was small it is supposed to have three quarters of a ton of breaking strain and I guessed that it would be OK. I had to find clothes, my oily trousers and boots, then buoyancy aid followed by oily jacket. As I struggled to put each one on I gradually warmed up and by the time I was kitted up I felt much less fear and more confidence, because I knew that I was now personally less vulnerable. If I ended up in the water I was better off, but what else did I need? I put two torches in my pockets because I knew that I stood no chance of being found without them. I switched on my mobile phone and hoped that I'd be able to get a chance to dial 999 whilst holding it above water to give my position. Could I get a signal round here?

Before the worst happened I would probably have to try to row, so the first essential would be to get the tent down. I could rip the poles apart and break the Velcro bonds, but the operation that would take the longest time would be releasing shackles used to attach parts of the tent higher up the standing rigging. I realised that standard screw-shackles would be far too slow. I needed the quick release of the captive-pin type, but even these can be tricky to line up in the dark. I made a mental note to change them if I survived. By mentally preparing for the worst and rehearsing courses of action I was increasing my readiness to deal with the shock of what might befall me. This has been shown to be an essential element in survival situations.

I now knew that I had to conserve as much energy as possible whilst monitoring what was happening outside. The movement was great, the noise continuous and I marvelled that the tent remained intact. I looked out of my windows to observe the lights on land, as they seemed to move back and forth due to the bucking and turning of the boat. I set up the oarlocks and readied the oars, then I lay down and chocked myself up to be able to see what was going on. The boat was holding steady so the anchor was OK, which was a relief. I began to wonder if I would be able to free it in the morning as it was getting such a severe workout.

I thought that it was important to occupy my mind to divert my attention away from the unsettling noise, so I got out my little radio, put in the earphones and found a station. Any station would do, just to take my mind away from where I was. At random I found a station where they were reading a story, which was a more effective mental distraction, than just plain music. When the story finished they moved onto weather reports and then the shipping forecast. It was a relief to hear that nowhere was supposed to be getting the extreme weather which was just the thickness of tent fabric away from me, trying to get in. It had to be a local effect and therefore, I reasoned, it couldn't last. In fact, although it remained strong it was becoming less gusty and more consistent. I began to relax, knowing that it could only be getting better. After another half an hour I felt that it would be alright to sleep again and when I awoke an hour or so later we were in smooth water as it had ebbed to being very shallow. I took off my oilies and scrambled back into my sleeping bag knowing that the worst had passed.

It was a salutary lesson that brought home to me how vulnerable I could be relying on the strength of a single piece of anchor line or how something as apparently unimportant as the type of shackle used on my tent might become the difference between safety and danger. I'm not a fan of all that 'Health and Safety' stuff that can intrude into our lives, but I had never done a serious 'Risk Assessment' on being in bed, in a tent, on a small boat, in a rising gale with the open sea to leeward and my safety hanging on that single thread. I didn't expect to be there, in that place of danger, but that did not give me any protection. Was I unlucky? Well sometimes you make your own luck. I could take some simple steps to improve my chances should there be a next time, such as having the torch and mobile phone (VHF etc.) in the *right place; by not burying the oars and ALWAYS following the safest procedure for protecting and securing to the ground tackle. I suppose you could ask a few questions about your own actions. Has the weather ever been bad enough to make you ask the question 'Should I wear my lifejacket in bed?' One day, quite unexpectedly, you might find yourself there. If you do, will you be ready for the answer?*

Quick! An antidote.
(It isn't always like this either.)

Renee and Jim Bailey lazy sailing their Devon Dayboat around a sunny Thames Estuary. 121/22

The weather was warm and dry. The wind died away in the evening, as we got the stove going, cooked our meal and brewed the tea. We were able to watch lots of waders dibbing in the mud banks for food. It turned into a lovely evening with a good sunset. Then it was up tent – we sat by the zip door till dusk.

Next day it was very hot and sunny all day long (cries of disbelief). Sunbathed all day, ate and drank when we wanted and went over the side for three swims. Lots of Dunlin and Curlew about and one lone Heron standing in the shallows hunting. All boats were away by the afternoon. We lounged and heard the tennis final. It was a lovely day and now we had the place to ourselves again – a good night's sleep.

The weather was hot and sunny again. We had a good sail and having tacked all the while landed at the Medway Yacht Club hard, filled our water containers, had a cuppa and signed their visitors book. Back to the boat for food and brew (I like tea, best drink in the world). The Club canteen lady's name is Dolly just in case you use the place – a lovely club with a superb view of the river. Oh! the sheer luxury of sitting there, seeing the world go by in the 'dimsey' watching the setting sun.

5.

Domestic Arrangements
and
Safety.

DCA Quotes.

'Finding this welcome little creek we got under the lee of its tiny peninsula and dropped the hook for a mug of tea and a silent thanksgiving. We had survived our toughest battle to date and dinghy cruising became our favourite sport once more.'
John Deacon.

5.
Domestic and Personal Equipment.

Inside.

Inside the boat tent there have to be living systems, rather as there are inside a land tent or even a house. You can't duplicate normal domestic systems; they have to be pared down to the barest essentials in order to save weight, but also to keep sufficient comforts to make the exercise sustainable. The main systems are:

1. Eating.
The Galley.
Cooking arrangements.
Storage of food and implements.
Water.
2.Sleeping.
The Bed.
Mattress and sleeping bag.
3. On-Board equipment.
Lookout List
The Toilet.
Washing.
Clothes storage.
Navigation.
4. Safety.

The Galley.

The kind of galley arrangements to be found in dinghies can vary. People cruise in different ways. On day-sails in rivers and estuaries close to centres of population some people will 'Bed and Breakfast' ashore, whilst others may seek solitude and may not even step ashore or speak to anyone for several days. Those who undertake long sea journeys live in a different world of working the boat, discomfort and fatigue, with the ultimate reward of adventure and achievement. Their catering is 'expedition eating' and not within the range of this book. The domestic patterns of each group will directly contrast with the others and their equipment will vary accordingly. Here I am concentrating on the factors to be considered when beginning to set up cooking arrangements on a cruising dinghy.

What did I do?

Eating.

Cooking Arrangements.

For my galley I started by deciding which fuel I would use, then took a stove on board together with a pan and some water and tried to make myself a cup of coffee whilst still attached to the mooring. I recommend that you do this; I learned a lot. What happened? Well first it might be a useful exercise to see how I decided which fuel I would favour, because many other cruisers use the various alternatives. I had the usual questions. Which is the best cooking fuel? Which should I use? **Personal researching is essential.**

Perhaps some facts and figures might help?

The DCA has some detailed information.

Dick Houghton. Solid fuel 191/57, Liquid fuel 192/45.

I also looked in a Field & Trek Catalogue (See 'Suppliers'), where each of the major fuel types, liquid fuel, gas and alcohol were analysed and their advantages and disadvantages reviewed in the technical section

These are my extracts from their information.

Speed.

In the test for boiling 1 litre of water the very best liquid fuel stove took 3 mins 35 secs and was almost a minute faster than any other similar fuel stove. The meths burner took 15 mins 45 secs. The standard Primus gas stove took 3 mins 45 secs.

Weight/Duration.

The liquid fuel stove weighed 6000 grams, whilst the Primus weighed 400 grams. On a tank full of fuel the gas stove lasted almost half as far again as the liquid fuel with times of 2 hours 50 mins. and 2 hours respectively.

Size.

According to the sizes given in the catalogue the gas stove took only one sixteenth of the space occupied by the liquid fuel stove.

Each of these is an important consideration, but there are others, such as fuel availability, ease of use, cost, speed of starting and ease of control. For me it was 'no contest', the gas stove was an easy winner when one considers the simplicity of the arrangement. 'Gas stoves are trouble free and durable.' said the catalogue. So why doesn't everyone use them as a matter of first choice?

The most frequently heard criticism is the familiar one of the danger of explosion in the boat, but as we are using it in an open dinghy, taking normal sensible precautions this should surely minimize that risk. Any flame constitutes a fire risk. It is not something that causes me excessive concern, but you will have to make up your own mind. In the meantime, I will return to my practical test of making a cup of coffee.

I found that the worst problem with the standard, simplest, old gas burner stove design was its lack of stability, especially with a pan or kettle on top. I proved through experience that the pan could be upset on a stove, by wave action whilst on a mooring in moderate wind against tide conditions. To spill a pan of near boiling water is very dangerous, so at the very least, always wear boots. In addition I thought that in open or breezy conditions there was a serious heat loss between flame and pan with a constant danger of the flame being extinguished. (The catalogue suggested some tips for improving gas-stove performance such as 'put lids on pans' and 'use a windshield', which confirmed my feelings about heat loss. (Another tip aimed at saving gas was to pre-warm the food can by putting it inside the shirt.) To sort out these difficulties I began to evolve some solutions.

Securing the stove. (See diagrams.)
I needed a supporting structure for the pan at the correct height above the stove and I needed some kind of shield to both stabilise the pan and direct the heat onto it, to minimise heat loss. I found that I could fit a single small plywood shelf at the height of my forward buoyancy tank which would not only support the pans but would give me a useful food preparation surface to work on and it would make sufficient length (taken together with the buoyancy tank) for it to be used as a bed space for one of my small children if required. A hole in the shelf allows the gas stove to be beneath it, heating a pan placed above it. The shelf is supported at its outer corner by a detachable leg dropped into the gap between floorboards so that it is rigid enough take a person's weight. It is secured on a ledge around the side of the boat by two small rotating cleats.

The pan stabilising shield I made from a standard circular biscuit tin that proved to be the perfect size. I cut the bottom of the tin away. The modified lid of the tin was used below the shelf to protect the timber from the heat of the stove and the body of the tin was dropped into place on top of the shelf to hold the pan and retain the heat. A slot in the rim of the tin engages with the pan's handle. The stove can be used at consistently lower flame settings thus reducing the level of heat transferred to the shelf. When it is to be used as a bed, the tin shield is removed and a plywood disc dropped into the shelf hole. This disc has other functions, especially

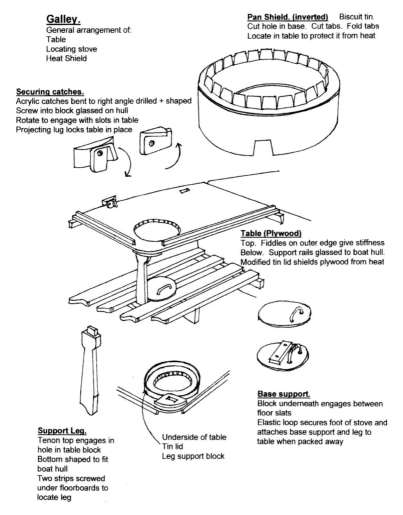

Galley.
General arrangement of:
Table
Locating stove
Heat Shield

Pan Shield. (inverted)   Biscuit tin.
Cut hole in base. Cut tabs. Fold tabs
Locate in table to protect it from heat

Securing catches.
Acrylic catches bent to right angle drilled + shaped
Screw into block glassed on hull
Rotate to engage with slots in table
Projecting lug locks table in place

Table (Plywood)
Top. Fiddles on outer edge give stiffness
Below. Support rails glassed to boat hull.
Modified tin lid shields plywood from heat

Base support.
Block underneath engages between
floor slats
Elastic loop secures foot of stove and
attaches base support and leg to
table when packed away

Support Leg.
Tenon top engages in
hole in table block
Bottom shaped to fit
boat hull
Two strips screwed
under floorboards to
locate leg

Underside of table
Tin lid
Leg support block

that of steadying the gas stove in use. It has wooden blocks on its underside that can be engaged between the floorboard slats below the stove. An elastic loop in it secures one of the stove's feet, to stop it sliding and prevent it from accidentally being knocked over.

The whole structure can be removed and clipped back against the inside of the boat when sailing. For storage the loose, circular metal pan shield fits neatly inside a plastic washing up bowl, nesting with the pans. I have spent time and space here describing the evolution of my cooking arrangement as it demonstrates how decisions should be based upon the knowledge gained from researching information. Since I evolved my solutions there have been advances in gas stove design and it is now possible to find better stoves on sale in camping shops as the manufacturers have addressed the very problems that I wrestled with when making my choices. Stoves are heavier, but acceptably so. They are stable, being housed in rectangular bases, with far superior gas

Keith Holdsworth using a flat stove.

Chris Waite's suspended stove.

replacement and control systems. They would be my starting point if I had to begin my investigations again. Other cruisers seem to favour 'box' systems for keeping the stove in, which gives stability and acts as a windshield.

Pans.

I looked in the camping shops at the nesting pan/containers but they were horrendously expensive. I could see that they were simple aluminium containers. What made them special were their handles that were detachable so that they would nest inside each other. They are a good product and they are widely and popularly used, but they are often rectangular and I wanted a circular shape.

As a 'dinghy cruiser' their cost was a challenge to me. When I went into a local chain store I saw sets of three small pans costing half of one 'camping shop' pan. They had conventional handles held on with a single screw. The detached handles of the pans were too long to fit inside the pan. One day I saw these cheap pans on offer at half price. I bought a set. On the two small pans I sawed a small surplus length off the handles and modified them to be easily removed from the pan. Pans, handles and lids now nest inside each other within the pan shield inside the plastic washing up bowl for compact storage. They are held in place by a thin, flat, plywood lid for the bowl that acts as a cutting/preparation board. The board has shaped edges so that it will pass through the hatch into the forward buoyancy tank for stowage. This whole assembly is held together with two webbing straps on a loop of shock cord.

Storage of food and implements.

Containers and checklists.
Different people have different methods for getting the multitude of items needed for cruising on board, but I have evolved this system that suits me and may prove a starting point for you. Organisation is important. Firstly, it is **essential** to have **checklists** and they need to be permanently attached to their relevant containers, otherwise you will be constantly struggling, because something has been forgotten.

My two most important sealable plastic containers contain my kitchen requirements. One is quite large 270 x 150 and 150 deep. This is because it holds my gas stove. It also allows me to have a couple of longish items in it:

A sharp kitchen knife (needed for bread and some meat)
A wooden spatula (lifting fried eggs)

Checklists are taped to the inside of containers but can be seen through the transparent sides. My list for this box is:

Stove, Spatula, Tea Towel, Wash up sponge, Torch little, Torch big, Scissors, Tin Opener, Beef-can key, Big Knife, Knife/Fork/Spoon.

After each journey I have to remove the sponge as its dampness rusts the stove fittings. The tea towel can be removed and then replaced before each journey.

My second container is only 170 x 130 and 70 deep and primarily it holds a variety of 'food substances'. For relatively short weekend or even week-long journeys I have found I will require only very small quantities of certain materials. Good examples might be washing-up liquid or tomato sauce. It is not necessary to carry complete bottles of these substances that would be too bulky and heavy. In this box I have some polythene containers once used for holding 35mm photographic film. They are labelled Salt, Cook Oil, Wash up, Ketchup, Mayonnaise. Other slightly larger containers have Sugar and Coffee. Also this box checklist has: Teaspoon, Lighter/Matches, and Kitchen towel (paper).

A third container has more general things, Toilet paper, Writing paper, Pen. Mini Flares, Radio/tape/batteries (Could be iPod / Mobile Phone / Camera etc.), Compass and Sunglasses. I check this, but do not always take all of the items in it. I have to keep my handbearing compass away from metal/magnets, but it has to appear on my checklists or it may be omitted.

Food. Be prepared.

Food containers/packets are stored in strong, different coloured, plastic shopping bags (Categorised as Fresh, Tinned, Eats for the Day.) that are going into buoyancy tanks. The bags make them easy to remove from the tank. Cheap thin shopping bags are needed to collect rubbish. I am not casual about the food quantities that are carried. Before leaving home I will list the days and the expected food for the cruise so that it may be partly pre-prepared. You may have to adopt a flexible attitude towards the whole process of the content of meals, storage, eating, and timings. The main reasons for careful planning are to save time, save weight and to undertake mundane tasks in conditions of maximum ease at home. Bread can be sliced, buttered and even spread with jam/marmalade, thus avoiding the need to carry tubs of margarine, jars of jam and filling the bilges with crumbs etc. I have often been grateful late at night, to eat marmalade sandwiches intended for a breakfast, when I have become too tired to prepare food because the journey has been prolonged or things have not gone according to plan. Meats, especially bacon or sausages can be cooked at home, cooled and stored in plastic containers. This saves on cooking fuel and a great deal of waiting for food on the boat.

Breakfast cereals can be carried in big margarine-tub type containers. Surplus cereal is decanted onto a plate then milk/sugar added to the cereal in the container as it makes a good lightweight bowl. After cleaning the container the remaining cereal is returned to it and the lid sealed down. Full cream milk lasts longer than skimmed. Sugar sweetened cans of drink or bars of chocolate give instant energy and need no preparation so they can substitute for a delayed meal if needed. In a similar way tinned 'all-day breakfast' or tinned rice pudding can be spooned straight from the can as instant meals, should conditions demand it.

Cup and Plate. Normal plastic ones will do, but I have ones that were originally designed to be used by babies. The cup has a spouted, push-on lid (teacher-beaker). It is fairly small but it doesn't spill and can be used in quite rough conditions when normal drinking would be difficult. The 'plate' is deep with vertical sides and can hold all foods, for all courses, without spilling.

Water.

Apart from people, this is the heaviest commodity (Approx. 10lbs per 5 ltrs) that is taken aboard, and you must take care not to carry too much of it. On a full sized cruising yacht the weight of the usual minimum allowance of half a gallon (2.5 ltrs) per day, per person, might be useful as ballast, but in a dinghy care should be exercised. Unless departing for very remote parts, you are rarely far away from a water supply and can get by in an emergency with much less than the full amount. Washing is curtailed anyway, other drinks are usually aboard and unless all food is dehydrated there should be little problem. Probably the biggest risk of running short might come from getting gale bound on a mooring for a while. I prefer to use fresh water rather than drag loads of stale, long-stored stuff around with me anyway. Some people will carry a medium sized, plastic soft drink bottle to top up, each time they go ashore, rather than take their main container.

I have the capacity to carry two 20 litre containers firmly secured in floorboard recesses tight against the centreboard casing, but I usually only have one in use. If I am going out alone for the weekend I will only have it just over half full, and I usually have enough surplus to wash the salt off the hull when I return. I have not yet heard of anyone dying of thirst whilst dinghy cruising. It is probably more critical and it will cause more of a problem to run out of cans of gas rather than to run low on water.

Sleeping.

The Bed.

Having arranged for an area large enough for a bed you also need a mattress and a sleeping bag. I found that for greatest comfort the bed platform should be raised above the floor level so that you can access it in the normal way and sit upright on its edge. If I make up my bed platform extended right across the boat it has to be accessed from the head end, involving (exhausting) squirming about and any sitting is done with straight legs, flat on the bed.

The Mattress.

The lightest solution for this is a cheap, thin, plastic blow-up airbed from almost any toyshop. Unfortunately they are not durable enough and subject to catastrophic failure in the middle of the night if they puncture. Two other points to be noted. They provide little insulation from below, but worst of all they take a long time and a lot of energy to inflate and deflate. There are much stronger cloth covered, inflatable mattresses that are acceptable for land/vehicle based camping, but they are exceedingly heavy for use on a boat and still take time to blow up and deflate.

Many backpackers use 'carry mats' of different types, some are like thin rolled sheets of insulation and others have an egg box-like structure. These do insulate from below and they are quick to deploy and recover but they are a bit hard to sleep on when lying on open-slatted, boat floorboard and they can be bulky when rolled. The ideal object that is required has a self-defeating specification. It needs to be thick and warm in use, yet compress into a tiny space and weigh nothing when being packed away.

Currently the best solution is the self-inflating mattress. This is a strongly made mattress with sponge-like foam inside its cavity. The inflation point is a valve on one corner. It is rolled tightly and the valve is closed. To use it, put it on the bed platform and unscrew the valve. The inner foam begins to reassert from its compressed state, sucking air in as the mattress slowly unrolls. A few minutes later you can add a couple of lungs-full of air to pressurize it and then seal the valve. There is very little effort. To deflate, open the valve and roll the mattress slowly from the opposite end. When it is rolled up, secure the valve again and replace it in its bag. The perfect solution? Well they are not cheap unless you buy a cloned copy, but they are worth the investment. Most camping shops stock Thermarest. Enter this into a search engine and you will get a range of suppliers. For the genuine article, make sure it is all one word. Clone-makers hyphenate the word for their similar products.

Sleeping Bag.

I knew very little about sleeping bags until I read the technical explanations in the Field and Trek catalogue (See lists at end of book) that explained the qualities of the different filling materials, cloths and sewing techniques. After a great deal of reading and comparing I found that some bags were half the price of others which were not too different, except that they carried a fancy name on the label. I realised that in a marine environment I should not use a down-filled bag, even if I had been able to afford it. Armed with real knowledge I was able to visit my local camping shops and sort out the genuine value items from those with 'designer labels'. One little problem with virtually all bags is that their stuff sacks tend to be short and fat rather than long and thin which is a better shape to pass through access hatches. I put my bag into a strong bin-liner type plastic bag with a drawstring top to keep it waterproof. When the mattress and the bag are stored at home they have to be in their uncompressed state.

For a pillow I take a normal pillowcase. As I remove my day clothes I fold them flat and put them into the case. This means that I always know where to find them the next morning, they remain warm and they are completely tidied away. In addition I have an inflatable pillow, which also goes in the pillowcase and when extracted, doubles as a cushion during the day to soften the hard seating in the boat. I have often described this cushion as the most vital piece of equipment in the boat, due to this additional function. This mention of hard seating brings me to an allied topic.

The Toilet.

This subject is not much written about, for a variety of reasons. One is that it is considered to be a little 'delicate' and there is no wish to offend anyone. Another is that it raises environmental issues and leaves those who discuss it, open to criticism if they admit to anything other than what is considered to be politically and environmentally correct.

My feeling is that talking about it, or not talking about it, does not fundamentally change what people have to do. We still all use toilet arrangements of one kind or another. So I will venture some thoughts which I hope may have some value and I will have to run the risk of censure.

As I see it, there are three main issues for the dinghy cruiser.
1. Where are we when we use the toilet?
2. How do we dispose of the waste?
3. What do we use and how do we use it?
It is difficult to separate these because each affects the other.

First, let me say that there is the totally honest and practical approach. I was once at a dinghy cruising meeting when this topic was raised and people were gently skirting around the issues when an elderly, very senior and greatly respected lady, interjected with the forthright assertion, "I don't really see what the problem is here. If I want to go, I simply hang out over the transom and have done with it."

Now she was well known for sea sailing and I think that for any craft alone at sea, such an approach would be practical, providing the waves were not too high and personal safety was not compromised. It might not find favour with absolutely everyone environmentally, but I think that we have to be realistic. In a marina it would raise some eyebrows, as it would on the river at the weekend. So the question of where we are, will determine, through commonsense and what other facilities are available to us, the methods that we use. Closed lakes and fresh water demand increased thought, care and responsibility.

Cruising dinghy sailors are few in number compared with the numbers of yachts with marine toilets on board, that in their turn, have an output which is miniscule compared with what the professional disposers put into the sea. This does not mean that we should not be sensitive to our responsibilities, but it does mean that there is a balance to be struck by each individual. Every creature other than human on the planet disposes of its waste as and where it wishes and the planet has evolved to utilise this process. It is mankind's success and concentrated living arrangements that are really causing the problem. So, the way that we dispose of the waste will depend on circumstances and the belief of each individual. It is possible to take everything back home and flush it down a toilet to be processed (we hope) in some way, although it is probably still true that in some places (I have seen it myself) this will mean it is conveyed untreated to the sea. To collect everything and take it ashore really means using a chemical toilet, and I have seen them on small boats.

Systems other than this usually involve what has always been called 'bucket and chuck it', though as I have just explained, you exercise judgment on where and when, you 'chuck it'. I believe that most dinghy sailors use this system. I also know that when it comes to solid waste, if it is possible, they will go ashore armed with a trowel and bury it.

This is not the end of the story because there are still design decisions to be made regarding the 'bucket'. In the first instance, let us consider liquid waste. 'The men have it easy', is a general complaint from the ladies, because men can casually use any available 'convenient' container and most people know this usually means the boat's bailer. Ladies too can partake of the bailer if is of a reasonably practical design (meaning dimensions). The problems lay not so much with the container, but with finding a modest degree of privacy and also a comfortable position within the boat when using it. If privacy is needed for more solid 'motions' in a seated position and going ashore proves too difficult, it is possible to drop anchor or make up to a mooring then lower the mainsail to act as a temporary cover wrapped around one's middle or shoulders, or alternatively to put up a cuddy. This takes time.

This also leaves the comfort problem. When we use a domestic toilet it is fixed at a normal seat height of about 450mm (18") and it is strong enough to take our weight. Anything higher or lower that cannot take our weight will cause us problems. The thin rim and handle of a normal bucket plus its lightness and instability can lead to discomfort. The system has to be refined somehow.

I looked around aboard my boat for a seating position that was the right height. The standard bucket depth of about 250mm (10") is too low, so I was looking to position it below another structure that could take the weight of a seated person. As I searched I did wonder if the centreboard casing might be used in some way. The slot could be used for liquid only. It would require the boat to be afloat and the centreboard would have to be down. Some kind of funneling arrangement (modified milk container with seat over?) would be needed at a comfortable height. Kneeling height for men is between 250 - 300mm (10"-12") whilst women always require the standard seat height.

It's not essential to use a bucket. In general it is too big to justify space on board unless it is being used to store something else such as an anchor or warp. I did not normally carry a bucket. A bucket is only a plastic container. I looked at plastic containers in DIY stores and I checked my other onboard requirements for containers that were not used for food etc. I decided that the minimum container dimensions required for toilet use were considerably smaller than a bucket and I purchased a rectangular box that could also double as storage for boat spares equipment. I made a small drop-in lid for the box.

Toilet Support board.
(Timber covered in G.R.P.)

Broad, flat horizontal surface with
recessed opening

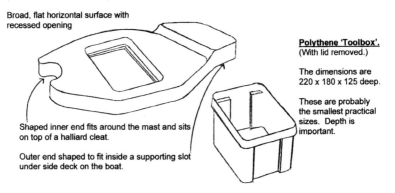

Polythene 'Toolbox'.
(With lid removed.)

The dimensions are
220 x 180 x 125 deep.

These are probably
the smallest practical
sizes. Depth is
important.

Shaped inner end fits around the mast and sits
on top of a halliard cleat.

Outer end shaped to fit inside a supporting slot
under side deck on the boat.

I took the box to the boat and again looked for a strong position at the right height. There was nowhere that was perfect. I considered making a supporting box around it that could rest upon the thwart, but this would have to be quite wide if it was to be sat upon. Eventually I decided to make a plank-like seat to bridge the gap from the underside of the coaming on one side of the boat across to the mast. In the centre of the plank I worked a recess into which the box could be dropped so that its rim would be level with the surface of the plank. To secure it on the mast at the correct height I moved one of the halliard cleats to allow the board to sit on top of it and I shaped a support at the side of the boat below the side deck. I took great care to eliminate all surplus weight from the board so that it is more like a frame and I covered it in a layer of GRP to strengthen it and make it fully waterproof.

When not in use, this support board clips against the side of the boat and the box is stored separately with its tools in a plastic bag inside it. This allows the box contents to be removed instantly (in their bag), and protects them from any seawater that might dampen the inside of the box after it has been washed out. It only takes a minute or so to put the box (with seawater in it) into the frame and position it in place alongside the mast. It feels almost 'normal' to use, as it is solid, strong and at the usual height. Doug Heslop 197/11 independently reached similar conclusions to mine, but used paper containers inside his box; his article has a clear, dimensioned diagram. There are possibly more efficient solutions, but I think that the world is waiting for an accomplished lady designer to design and develop the appropriate equipment.

As my tent is curtained across the middle into two spaces it is possible to have a degree of privacy if it should be required when living aboard with a companion. Anyone taking up dinghy cruising must recognise that in such a small space, toilet arrangements will have to be considered early (before sailing), if embarrassment is likely and has to be avoided.

On-Board Equipment.

Acquire these things.
When you are concentrating on the practicalities of working on the boat you tend not to think too deeply about other things that you will need. When the time comes to put the cruising exercise into effect you find that you really ought to have been gathering some stuff together as you went along. Some items, such as pans, you can borrow from the kitchen, temporarily, but as you will have noticed, from what I have written, it sometimes helps to study other requirements and keep a general **'lookout'** for what you will eventually need. If there is time to pick and choose, you can sometimes buy a better article, or one that is just the right size or weight. You can buy in a 'Sale' or get it as a 'gift'. Just before I present my 'lookout list' of mainly domestic items, I should mention again the DCA Boat Safety Recommendations. This covers a number of the items below and mentions one or two others also. I will include a condensed version of the 'Recommendations' for comparison, following my list.

Lookout List.
(Already mentioned.)   A cooking device, some pans, crockery, cutlery. Try to avoid borrowing from home because something always gets forgotten. Having dedicated utensils that stay in their boxes or on the boat gets rid of such problems.
Food and water containers
Sleeping bag. Pillow. Mattress
Clothes. You normally sail with what you stand up in and minimum spares. I have a small 'drysack' about 150mm diameter and 500mm long inside and I restrict my spare clothes to this size. It's important to have good waterproof 'oilies' to wear, but you do want them to be as lightweight as possible. This is not too easy to find cheaply. I wear a buoyancy jacket at all times until my tent is erected and I have settled down. Similarly I put it on before starting to dismantle the tent. It's good for keeping me warm at all times. I have to wear

an oilie jacket big enough to go over the top of my buoyancy vest. The vest has crotch straps. Very important, wear a sunhat.

Boots / Trainers. If I wear my sailing boots whilst sailing I never lose the feeling that I am 'daysailing'. I wear them, of course, when it is raining or when taking spray on board, but I like the 'luxury' of changing into my trainers once I am clear of the shore in sheltered waters. It's my little signal to myself that I am now 'living aboard' and wearing 'normal' shoes. I feel a bit the same about the oilie top and prefer to wear some kind of fleece or padded jacket in dry conditions, especially after I have stopped sailing and I am just 'living' aboard.

A possessions bag for the clothes. Drysacks are strongly welded PVC bags sealed across their rolled-up top with Velcro and secured with clips. They are available from chandlers. I have a big one and a small one. They need some quick method of securing them firmly to the boat so they can act as additional buoyancy and can't get lost. The Velcro at their entrance makes it difficult to put woolly jumpers or fluffy towels into them. If you subdivide your clothes into cheap plastic carrier bags they slide past the Velcro and you can then use another carrier bag for storing dirty washing.

Your personal washkit bag. The usual but small quantities of soap, toothpaste/brush, medications, creams etc. For a shaving mirror I use one retrieved from a woman's powder compact.

First Aid kit. To some extent the contents are going to be a matter of personal choice. Mine contains a needle and a craft knife blade for example, as well as some items which are no longer 'recommended' but which I like, such as the old 'fabric' Elastoplast (they give abrasion protection) and antiseptic cream. I think it is important to have insect bite cream and something to zap mosquitoes with. Headache pills etc. need replacing periodically. Standard kits in nice green boxes are sometimes a bit big, with bandages suitable for a hospital ward, so you have to check them out and think for yourself. The most important thing is to fasten the box where it can be accessed in a hurry, singlehanded.

Fire. What are you doing about this? It's your choice. It is especially important if you carry outboard fuel. You may also have guidance if you have an insurance policy or you are licensed to travel on an inland waterway as there will be set minimum standards that you must obey.

A tool kit. This is a bit like the First Aid Kit. You can drag aboard a mass of weighty kit but still not have what you want when the time comes. The best overall advice is to have a well-maintained boat

(See 'Maintenance') to minimise the chances of gear failure. For 'Spares' I allow myself one small screwtop container holding various screws, shackles, clevis pins, split pins etc. and a small bag of bits of 'string' of various lengths. When it comes to tools I never go sailing without a small pair of 'Mole' or 'Vise grips'. I even like two pairs.

A small screwdriver with interchangeable bits.

A small 'Junior' hacksaw. It saws both wood and metal and sometimes bread!

Rolls of plastic sticky tape.

These are my basics. After this it is personal choice.

Plastic trowel. Explained in 'Toilet' (but you probably guessed).

Brush and dustpan. Keeping the inside of a boat clean is a constant domestic chore made much more difficult by shore visits, in particular, to sandy beaches. If the family eats a picnic lunch on board there will be all manner of food accumulating in the bilge. A normal brush and dustpan is too big to get into the odd shaped bilge corners so I use a smaller set, actually sold as a children's toy, which is most effective.

Lighting. LEDs have transformed this problem. There are some excellent fold-down lanterns now. Wind-ups are great, head beams good and modified solar powered garden lights are popular especially as riding lights if needed. I still like the small torch that I can hold in my mouth when required. Know exactly where you keep it, so that you can find it immediately when waking at night.

My approach for Navigation/Pilotage.

For my kind of sailing (which requires mainly pilotage) I check my charts at home before sailing and where appropriate I copy relevant information, sometimes changing its size to make it bigger, or all the same scale. I stick pieces together from different places to make one total picture. I write onto the 'charts' I have thus made all the important details, such as tide times and tidal differences etc. This means that I do not have to carry my large expensive charts and heavy almanacs etc. When afloat I work out what I have to do prior to sailing each day. I have no chart table, nor specialist navigating equipment. I use a bearing compass suspended on a thin line around my neck and I take periodic sightings when necessary. Offshore work would need a different approach. As an experienced sailor I usually have prior knowledge of the areas I am sailing. I do not usually carry personal GPS/Chartplotter but many dinghy sailors do and I would recommend them for sea passages.

Each person will decide whether they want a mobile phone/ VHF or not. I do have a personal/pocket radio/tape player (it's old technology, but worth almost nothing and therefore expendable in case of accident) for news, weather and a little entertainment. This has been of good use when (for a variety of reasons) I have had to keep an eye on my situation during the night and had to stay awake. I need to ensure that my shirt has a good-sized breast pocket for carrying the device. The other use for this pocket is to keep a box of safety matches warm and dry in it, if they are used.

Storage areas.
As I have said, in general I use the forward buoyancy tank for food and domestic gear. The aft tank is for boat equipment tools, ropes, spares etc. I also have a plastic box secured (like a drawer) on the underside of a side seat for 'day access' to things like sun cream, sunhat, camera, sandwich, a drinks can and a chocolate bar. This makes them easy of access, without disturbing other storage areas.

A Warning about all these things.
Look at their volume. Feel their combined weight. It is amazing how 'stuff' accumulates. Never forget that 'Possessions expand to fill the storage space available'. Always be asking yourself 'How can I reduce this stuff, in volume and weight?' Every time you leave the boat think about what you can take away. Find anything that you didn't use this time and question whether you will really need it next time?

DCA Boat Safety. (Edited) Outline Recommendations.

The Boat.
A. The boat should be stable enough to allow the recommended weight of crew (20kgs/metre, 14 lbs for each foot of waterline length, suggested as a minimum) to sit on the gunwale without dipping it under or capsizing the craft. Stability is usually achieved with hull shape and/or ballast.
B. The boat should carry sufficient tested buoyancy to support itself with stores and partially immersed crew, plus reserve of not less than (50kgs). This buoyancy should be so disposed that it is possible for the crew to put the boat back into sailing condition after capsizing or swamping.
C. Mast, rigging, fixtures and fittings etc
Each of these must be in good repair and strong enough to withstand capsizing forces.

D. Sails. The mainsail should be capable of being reefed and the foresail reduced/ changed down whilst at sea.

E. Structures at the bow should shed incoming water overboard to avoid swamping in open and ballasted boats.

F. There should be a tested means to enable the crew to get aboard from being in the water.

G. The Crew. The crew should have knowledge and experience appropriate to the nature of the sailing being undertaken.

H. Equipment. At least one correct-sized Lifejacket / Buoyancy jacket, plus waterproofs and warm clothes for each crewmember.

Stopping.
At least one anchor and associated tackle appropriate to the craft's location. A strong painter of adequate length, firmly attached and securing warps.

Propulsion. Two metal oarlocks secured to the vessel and a pair of oars of adequate length / strength for sustained rowing. (Paddles are not a satisfactory substitute.)

Bailing. A strong bucket and bailer secured with lanyards, and/or pumps of equal efficiency.

Functioning means of attracting attention. Powerful light conforming to Collision Regulations. Pyrotechnic distress signals. An audible device. Modern communications device.

Safety. Have aboard. Appropriate navigational devices. Boat repair kit / tools. Firefighting device. First Aid kit. Sufficient food and drinking water. Adequate sun protection.

I. Actions. Prior to any journey, appropriate people ashore should be informed of intentions, expected arrival times and communications agreed. Register with Coastguards, Form CG6.

DCA Boat Safety Recommendations.
(Edited) Additional Explanatory notes.
Len Wingfield has done a great deal of boat safety work and experimentation over many years. These are some extract from his writings, which repeat, reinforce and sometimes modify most of what I have said, as well as adding to this very important topic.

Dinghy Cruising is an adventure activity. It has hazards that study, training and experience can reduce to an acceptable level. Formal training is valuable but experience is also a most vital factor. An ability to swim should be a pre-requisite followed by an ability to sail well in sheltered waters. Sailing on tidal or estuarine waters greatly increases the potential dangers, whilst sea sailing (coastal voyaging) and ultimately open sea crossing should never be undertaken without a high degree of training, skill and experience.

Generalising about the wide range boat types is not easy. Lightweight open craft and heavily ballasted craft have cruised successfully. Crews have ranged from several heavyweight athletes to singlehanded octogenarians. The following notes are therefore to be considered as a general guide.

The Boat.

Hull. The stability of a heavy hull with a generous waterline beam can also be achieved in other hull configurations, multihulls for example and also, with or without the addition of ballast. The crew should not need to sit out continuously.

Swamping. Open dinghies should have a foredeck with washboards or a similar cover capable of deflecting water overboard.

Consideration should be given to the problem of getting back into the boat following capsize or swamping. Testing one's boat in sheltered conditions is strongly advised. (A very informative article 194/47 by Len Wingfield has invaluable advice based on testing and practical experience.) It should be stressed that capsizing is not an acceptable proposition in a seaway due to the long period of exposure that may ensue and the possible loss of stores and equipment. In rough seas recovery can become impossible. Rope strops, ladders, fixed lines and rudder slots are some methods worthy of consideration and experiment. Any arrangement should have been tested.

Mast, Rigging, Fixtures and Fittings. Stainless rigging should be examined and replaced at regular intervals as it can fatigue/fail without warning. Ten years is reasonable for a well-used boat. All equipment, Rudder, tiller, ropes and board should be in good repair.

Engine. Outboard motors can be a great asset but they should never be used as a substitute for sailing skills. The crew should always have the ability to substitute manual for mechanical power.

Crew skills.

It is not possible to define all the separate areas of knowledge for each individual in every location. The simplest advice would be that the contents of the RYA Competent Crew and Day/Coastal skipper courses should provide a firm foundation of knowledge. In addition there are elements of the RYA's dinghy sailing scheme such as capsize and recovery which it is important to know (Capsize Testing Made Easy. Len Wingfield 194/47). Dinghy cruisers need to

Len conducting experiments.

conform to SOLAS regulations. On board reference cards for Collision avoidance, First Aid and RLNI rescue etc. should be considered. It is most important that all processes of sailing/boat handling can be undertaken at all times by those on board whilst still afloat.

Human factors. Both helm and crew need stamina. Try to plan the cruise to restrict sea time to no more than four hours at one time. Crews should be aware of their own sailing limits but in any case be prepared to abandon, postpone or seek shelter on receiving a forecast greater than F 5.

Equipment.
<u>Stopping.</u> Main Anchor. If Fisherman type, 1.5kg per metre of overall length. Bruce, CQR, Danforth types 1kg per metre. Anchor warp 30 metres minimum length, non-floating material. 8mm is an average size. 2 – 3 metres of chain attached to anchor. The bitter (inner) end to be secured to a strongpoint. A second anchor and warp made up. Normally lighter than main anchor.

A painter minimum (10 metres x 8mm) firmly secured and able to be lead through a strongly fixed bow fairlead.

<u>Means of attracting attention.</u> In addition to a powerful light conforming to Collision regulations there should be at least one other torch.

Pyrotechnic signals should be in date, in waterproof packs.
A loud horn or whistle can give the audible signal.
Consider manual alternatives to devices relying on compress air.
Communications device. VHF. Mobile Phone or other devices are a matter of personal choice. Protect from water.
They can be as useful in stopping a search, as in instigating one.
Safety. Navigational devices. A reliable compass checked for deviation if fixed. A pocket / bearing compass. Sufficient charts, pilotage/tide table information for the journey being undertaken.
Means of plotting a course and fixing position, including GPS.
A simple lead line marked in metres.
A radio device capable of receiving weather/shipping forecasts, protected from water.
Repair kit, tools and spares as required for the boat/engine.
A fire blanket and/or extinguisher, dependent on equipment carried.
First Aid kit + instructions (read beforehand and use as reminder).
Food and drinking water. Water 1.5 litres/person/day, plus spare.
Sun hat, sunglasses, sun cream.

SOLAS V. Since 2002 some regulations have been in force concerning the **S**afety **O**f **L**ife **A**t **S**ea. Before setting out in a boat you should be aware of the content of the regulations and how they might relate to you. The full text might be too much (available on mcga.gov.uk/publications) so check through boating organisations to find out what is there.

Similarly there is an International Convention for Prevention of Pollution from ships (MARPOL) that informs you that you cannot discharge oil or dispose of rubbish at sea.

Do you know your Col Regs? (Collision Regulations).

The free RNLI **Sea Safety CD-ROM** (if available) gives practical moving examples to inform you and to test your knowledge.

These are just examples (*See information at end of book*).

<u>Never be complacent about your sailing knowledge.</u>
<u>Always seek to learn more.</u>

Capsize.
For a number of years there was a single response to the question of capsize within the DCA and that was 'Don't'. The advice was good, but it still left an uneasy feeling and little reassurance. Capsize is a wide ranging subject, Who? How? Why? Where? Actions? Assistance? Avoidance? What boat? What equipment?

Regrettably I cannot go into all that is required to cover the subject properly. It merits another book to deal with everything. I can offer some instant advice based, as usual, on experience. If you have not been deposited into cold water with your clothes on, then you should arrange a way to experience it in safely-controlled circumstances. The older you are, the more important this is. The most dangerous part is what is called 'cold shock'. You find yourself gasping and unable to breathe. It doesn't matter how good a swimmer you once were, you'll be totally surprised and even panicked by what feels like a severe asthma attack. You need your buoyancy aid/lifejacket for those first few minutes, just until your lungs begin to work again. The next advice is to know what to do. You MUST have at least run through the 'Righting Procedure', read it or seen it done. You **must** understand the process and so must anyone else with you. In recent years the hard line attitude (or is it denial?) of 'Don't' has been softened as members have discussed ways for returning on board from a 'man-overboard' situation (looped ropes, steps in rudder blades, Len Winfield 194/47) or have conducted tests and experiments by voluntarily capsizing and righting their boats. Some have recorded the event in pictures or made modifications to their craft as a result. Commercial craft builders have used computers to simulate capsize and then built self-righting qualities into their products. The whole subject has become one that is being addressed and solutions are being sought. Whatever your attitude you bear a powerful responsibility to learn about and gain experience of capsize. Not because you will be going out there to capsize, but simply because you will be placing yourself in a situation where capsize will be a possibility and if it should happen, your best hope of dealing with it will be that you have properly prepared your boat, your companions and yourself for that eventuality. Essential-reading, capsize accounts. Peter Whyman 82/12. John Baden 97/08. Keith Muscott 206/58. Capsize pictures 201/ 37-40 & account Matthew Cunningham 202/37, 43+44. 217/43 Miles Dent. Buoyancy pocket in sail 215/42 Abela.

Testing All Systems.
Trial and Error.
All the work of making things, testing things and gathering things together takes quite some time. Sooner or later it all has to be tested. The tent can be put up in the dinghy park. Can it be put up in the dinghy park from inside the boat only, without ever stepping on the ground? Can it then be put up with the boat on a mooring?

Or riding to an anchor? This is the way that it goes. Each step has to be tested. Modifications have to be made. It can be a slow, but enjoyable process testing out your ideas. Will they work?

When the solutions that I have arrived at are presented for you to read, it may look as though I had a single solution to each design challenge and it was perfect and it worked first time. Nothing could be further from the truth. I am just as much a bungler as anybody else. I think that I now know, what I know, because I made every possible mistake along the road to knowing it. Many things that I have already included here were discovered the 'practical' way, as may be illustrated by another little story of an early cruise. Prior to this I had already tested all systems for myself, but I had not included the family. So what happened when I took them for the first time? Another cautionary tale.

A Place for Everything.
Departure.

It was an early experiment. Could we do an overnight cruise and a camp ashore with mum and dad and two young boys in our 13ft dinghy? The first discovery was that the loading limit for the boat was determined by the height of the water inside the centreboard casing. It was amazing just how much kit we could pack into that boat. Another limit seemed to be how much gear we could carry from the car park to the dinghy park, which was quite a distance.

When we did set sail she felt like a keelboat rather than a dinghy, but she carried it all extremely well. Surprisingly, in the light and fluky patches we left other dinghies behind, due to our inertia. Once we cleared the worst wind shadows we held them off due to our increased stiffness. I was really proud of her performance, overloaded as she was with food and water, bedding and clothes for four, her own tent and another tent to go on shore.

An hour's sailing against the tide down the river found us landing at high water on our sheltered beach at the head of a broad, shallow bay. It was 3 o'clock on a bright sunny afternoon. For an hour we unloaded and explored and tried to erect the shore tent with pegs into soft sand. Half unloaded and with gear strewn all around us I couldn't find the saucepans that had been temporarily stored in a bucket, so they should have been easy to spot. We changed from casual, disjointed activities to a detailed search, but no, they weren't with us. I could only think that I must have left them, when loading, tucked under an adjoining boat in the dinghy park. Not having them meant no cooking; a serious blow to the venture. The ebbing tide had now left the dinghy clear of the water. It was time for the inventive mind of the dinghy cruiser to save the day. We worked out that if we opened the tinned sweetcorn and peaches first, we could decant the contents and cook in the tins, holding the can with a 'tin-opener' handle. Further discussions confirmed we would manage, somehow.

I turned from this setback to erecting the dinghy tent, an impressive array of interlocking poles and clips. They were all in place. The sail cover was on, the halliards and mainsheet were rearranged and the jib was in it's bag when I turned to pick up the tent canopy ... in it's bag ... which...was...? Nowhere to be seen? I suddenly knew that it was with the pans. I knew not precisely where, but it was likely to be in the dinghy park, somewhere. What a total disaster. No time for further discussions. There was no overland connection from this remote spot and the water in the river was fast disappearing. There was no help by telephone to kindly relatives. We could hardly all sleep in one two-man tent...
Return.
I had no alternative but to sail back for the tent (and the pans). I had to get the boat back into the receding water quickly before the soft mud of the bay stopped me from getting away.

A period of panic is the time to take the greatest care. Leaving the shore presented the strongest possibility of being unable to return due to the softness of the mud preventing me from getting access again until near high water. Whilst I scrambled to unload the rest of the clothes, water and equipment I had to take care that I had sufficient to ensure my own needs should I become grounded on a mud bank for the night. I was concerned about getting my protective oilies and lifejacket aboard. My wife was reloading cake into the boat to ward off hunger (and scurvy) maybe? It would probably come in handy after midnight.

My boat rollers are cruiser fenders and useful pieces of equipment. They break the suction of the sand and mud on the bottom of the boat, making it seem only half the weight. With all the stores ashore the boat was considerably lighter anyway so following a muddy struggle I got her to the water's edge. Once afloat I had to re-rig her whilst my anxious wife stood marooned with her little boys, surrounded by a 'shipwrecked' of stores scattered along the tide line of the lonely beach.

With oar and sail I made good time working back up against the ebb using the failing evening breeze until eventually I made it right back to the launching ramp at the dinghy park and secured the boat. I scrambled over the seawall to my place in the dinghy park, to find ... nothing. No bucket? No tent? I began searching and eventually discovered them near to the entrance of the compound. I remembered now. My arms had been aching from carrying excessive equipment from the car and the flimsy handles of the plastic supermarket bags had stretched to their limit. I'd had to put a couple of things down, intending to return for them. Under the pressure of getting the expedition afloat they had been overlooked.

I rushed everything back to the boat, now on the very end of the slipway and tossed them aboard to set off back without delay. I still had to hurry to try to beat the ever-exposing mudflats. I had the tide and wind in my favour and sailed back in record time.

At a distance from the beach it looked reasonably promising. The water wasn't incredibly low, but as I approached, the centreboard began touching the bottom and I had still quite a way to go. I retracted it and took to the oars, eventually coming to rest maybe about a hundred metres from the ribbon of sand on the shore where the family was watching. So near and yet so far. Decision time. Should I stay here? I pushed a testing blade of the oar into the ooze. It just sank deeper and deeper then stuck with the suction. I decided to keep my options open for just one more move. I tried to row off only to find myself virtually stuck. It took some spirited mud-rowing to get clear and afloat again.

My final option lay with the two horns of the bay. Being composed of more solid ground they might afford a closer approach to the land. Looking at them I had time for only one choice. I chose the upriver one and rowed towards it. After some exploring I managed to find a landing place to pull the boat aground and set its anchor. A long walk carrying the bucket of pans brought me at last to our beach camp.

Night.

Later that night, one wide-eyed seven year old boy and his daddy had a great adventure when they awoke aboard their dinghy, in a tent at three o'clock in the morning, pulled in the anchor, pinned up the edges of the tent and began rowing across bay. The moon shone a spotlight beam onto the black water haunted by a pale mist that drifted in patches just above the surface. Bird sounds from heron, owl and oystercatcher filled the still night air as the rhythmical creak of the oars and faint chuckling of the water marked the passage of their boat. From afloat the water looked to lap at the very door of the shore tent. The anchor was reset in the sand alongside it, to conclude the adventure.

Alongside many other things I learned that even the best checklist isn't good enough unless it checks that all the items are on board. Probably, a place for everything and everything in its place <u>aboard the boat</u> is the most effective checklist for dinghy cruising.

<u>My ways are not the only ways.
There are many ways, including your ways.</u>

As we briefly mentioned night sailing, let's take a look at another 'snapshot' (*taken in the dark*), of a rather more ambitious small boat (*check its size, 12ft*) crew 'surprised' to be the only boat launching at this time of night. (*Don't do this at home.*) Perceptions of danger have changed these days, but it is interesting to read about how things were done in the early days. This is a wide estuary at this point and this can easily be considered to be an open sea crossing.

<u>Roger Hadlee and Dick Sutcliffe practice night navigation
(Before GPS). 83/19
Open clinker dinghy 12' 3". No engine.
Bradwell towards Brightlingsea, River Blackwater.</u>

We launched at 20.35, rather surprised that we were the only boat on the water. Dick who has ambitions as a navigator had worked out a bearing from the chart on the Nass Beacon at West Mersea island, but we could not see it. Eventually we saw a light which Dick declared must be it, but it seemed too far north when taking a transit with the lights on East Mersea. Indeed this proved to be the case because when we eventually came up to it, it turned out to be a street lamp on the end of East Mersea (so much for our night navigation skills). We decided to follow the shoreline clearly visible by the light of the full moon. This enabled us to get a good slant towards Brightlingsea and it was very exhilarating and relaxing after a busy week in London to glide along over the calm sea with a shaft of moonlight on our beam – Turner would have been in his element. We arrived in Brightlingsea half an hour after midnight.

6.

Other equipment for Dinghy Cruisers.

DCA Quotes.

'I was up before the alarm and rowed quietly out amongst the silhouettes of moored craft. The silence was broken only by the marsh birds calling as the day approached. The purples and reds of sunrise reflected on the water.'

Alan Glanville.

6.
Rigging and Covers.

Mast and standing rigging.

For most dinghy sailors putting the mast up and down usually happens once a year at the beginning and the end of the season, but not so for camping cruisers. Tall alloy masts need some special measures if they are to be erected shorthanded. Keith Muscott 192/48, Campbell/Sluce 193/61 address basic mast raising problems. Owners of Wayfarers and Wanderers will have built-in tabernacles to make the process more manageable. I was lucky because as I have mentioned, my boat has the Gunter rig, which uses a small mast that is easily handled for storing in the boat when trailing and raising single-handed. A gaff that is set vertically above it then extends the mast. The gaff also fits inside the boat and this makes for a very simple arrangement that is easy and convenient.

If there is a problem it will come with the lengthy process (using clevis pins and split rings) of connecting the stays to the boat. I use carbine hooks on the ends of my standing rigging. After placing the mast in its step on the keel I only have to lean it backwards a little and snap the shroud carbine hooks onto their deck fittings. I move to the bow and attach the forestay carbine hook that is part of a downhaul system. I pull the downhaul and the rig is tensioned. When I sail inland I can extend the downhaul line to be secured on the deck, back near the shrouds. This effectively allows me easy access to the forestay tension so that I can release it and slope the mast backwards for low bridges. For extreme cases I can take the mast/rig down, then row and put everything back up again, all from within the boat. It is not difficult, just time consuming and needs care to avoid tangles and snags. (Sailhead buoyancy. Len Wingfield 127/34)

Making covers.

Removing my mast, gaff and boom allows me to store them inside the boat when the boat is not in use. This protects the sails, the gear and all the varnished wood, which saves me a great deal of maintenance. Perhaps even more important is what will follow from not having a standing mast. All dinghies need covers when they are ashore and the primary source of leaks in covers is the area around the necessary mast collar and sealing system across the foredeck. I do not have this problem. I have a plain all-over cover of a design so simple and effective that I have used it on several craft. With the

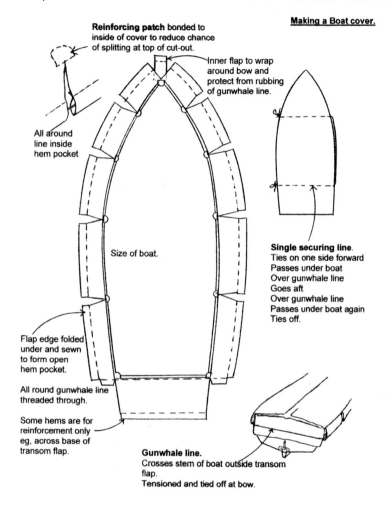

Making a Boat cover.

Reinforcing patch bonded to inside of cover to reduce chance of splitting at top of cut-out.

Inner flap to wrap around bow and protect from rubbing of gunwhale line.

All around line inside hem pocket

Size of boat.

Single securing line.
Ties on one side forward
Passes under boat
Over gunwhale line
Goes aft
Over gunwhale line
Passes under boat again
Ties off.

Flap edge folded under and sewn to form open hem pocket.

All round gunwhale line threaded through.

Some hems are for reinforcement only eg, across base of transom flap.

Gunwhale line.
Crosses stem of boat outside transom flap.
Tensioned and tied off at bow.

onset of winter the cover demonstrates another huge advantage over the conventional type where the mast must remain standing to maintain the cover's rain-shedding properties. Winter gales can blow boats over, so the most sensible precaution would be to remove the mast to reduce windage and store it, but this means the cover loses its support and the boom cannot maintain the cover tension. The result is a slack cover with a mast hole in it that simply gathers water instead of rejecting it. My overall cover could act as a winter cover for any boat without a mast. This would enable mast removal and proper maintenance checks, together with a dry boat and less deterioration. It is so simple to make that I will outline the general principles here. There is a message here. It doesn't have to be complex. Figure out what to do, and then add 'Simplicity'.

Practical. To make a boat cover.

- A central wooden beam runs from front to back of the open area (cockpit). In my Torch this beam is the mast. It could possibly be the gaff or boom?
- The outer edges of the cloth are folded over (100-150mm) to make a pocket for a drawstring that will pass right around the boat.
- The edge of the folded cloth may be glued in place. Gelled (*like Vaseline)* Contact Adhesive. (Thixofix, some Evostick.)
- It can then be sewn. (Big needle/sailmakers needle and thin, No. 4 whipping twine.) Draw a pencil line for the stitching to follow.
- Reinforcing patches may be glued/sewn to the inner end of the dart slots.
- A continuous line is threaded through the pockets, beginning and ending at the bow. It passes across the outside of the transom flap. The two ends are left quite long to avoid losing them into the pockets.

The mast or beam is placed on the boat. The cover is put on and the drawstring pulled tight below the gunwhale and tied off with a double bow.

- A single rope (blue polypropylene will suffice) is tied to the drawstring in one dart slot towards the stern. It passes under the boat, loops over the drawstring on that side, is pulled tight and carried forward to pass back into a dart slot over the drawstring nearer the bow. It is passed under the boat once more, tightened and made off to the drawstring again. To release the cover, this rope simply needs untying at its two ends and then the ends are pulled under the boat and laid across the top of the cover, which rolls back from the bow once the drawstring is released.

The boat has two other 'covers' (as well as the tent), that might be mentioned at this point.

The extended foredeck cover or deflector. (See 'Bailing' Ch 4.)
In addition to what I have said already:

- This deflector needs to be held up at the mast otherwise it could collect a weight of water that would depress it to form a puddle instead of shedding it overboard. It has a line attached to it that goes up to a barrel cleat on the front of the mast.
- The back edge has to be supported where it crosses the cockpit. This support must be inside the arc of movement of the kicking strap to allow it to remain in place and operational. I used a curved bamboo pole and a couple of bent metal tubes with dowels inserted to seal their outer ends. The dowels locate in oarlock sockets that were already part of the boat.
- The painter secured on the foredeck cleat has to be led back over the top of the cover and into the boat to remain usable.

In use, the Velcro mast collar prevents easy access to all halliards on the mast. Additionally, the support stick and cover make it difficult to reach the bow to pick up a mooring. This means getting prepared as the boat approaches the end of sailing. I peel off the Velcro flap at the mast and I dislodge the ends of the support stick from the sockets in the deck. This is all that is required. The cloth becomes flexible enough to move out of the way yet remains roughly in the right place with the stick attached. It can be quickly re-rigged if required, either when sailing or to deflect heavy rain.

A cockpit cover.
If you are cruising there is a strong possibility that you will want to go ashore and leave the boat for shopping trips or to visit places of interest. You may find yourself in the middle of a town or village and leaving your open boat with all of your equipment on display may not be the most sensible thing to do. Most of the time everything will be alright; the majority of people are totally trustworthy, but it is not wise to leave temptation in the way when it might be avoided.

I have a very lightweight blue polypropylene cover with hooks around the edge that can be attached to the tent lines below the gunwhale. It is lightweight because I prefer not to permanently carry items of excessive weight that are rarely used. It extends from the transom to the foredeck cover and simply hides all the loose contents of the boat. It gives me some peace of mind when I leave the boat tied alongside in places strange to me. It has a modification that makes it a bit like the spraydeck of a canoe. A hole with a vertical 'sleeve' positioned above the middle of the thwart allows me to rig it around my waist when I am rowing in rain and virtually windless conditions. The open area of a boat cockpit can collect a lot of water and this cover controls that situation. It is a bit like having one of those big, old-fashioned cycle capes that protected both the rider and the bike.

Practical Construction.

The DIY store, protective plastic sheet (blue polyprop) I used was for general gardening/building. All edges were turned and glued.
Eyelets were set at about 500mm.
Hooks folded with pliers from sections of wire coat hangers were attached with thin line to the eyelets.

Trolley and Trailer.

When first contemplating dinghy cruising there is a tendency to concentrate your thoughts on the boat and it is only gradually that you come to realise that if you are intending to use one of the major advantages of cruising in a dinghy, namely the mobility that it allows, you are going to need other major pieces of equipment and somewhere to keep them.

Standard class boats are often bought and sold along with their own trolleys and trailers. If you have a boat you may already have them. Otherwise, trailer manufacturers will be able to supply all that is needed for virtually any kind of dinghy, but it will come at a price. Another consideration is your car. Is it powerful enough? Does it have a towing hitch fitted? Are you familiar with towing legislation? Practically speaking, how good will you be at reversing the trailer into a tight space? Are you physically fit enough to launch and recover the boat?

Oh dear! This may be getting you into areas that you had not contemplated and it can be enough to put anybody off. I am not going to try to give the answers here. I cannot tackle such a large topic but I wanted you to be aware that the problems are there. If you are going to trail the boat you will have to begin some practical investigations to absorb relevant information when the opportunity arises and maybe get some towing practice somehow?

What did I do?

You will have seen in my 'Lost and Found' story that when I retrieved my boat I *'took it home on a borrowed trailer'*. My eldest son helped me. If you have to buy a boat you may find yourself in a similar situation to mine. This may be your first step too. Loading

Trolley, Trailer and Balance.

The dinghy on its launching trolley.

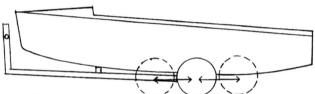

The wheel is a balance point.
If it is too far forward, the boat tips backwards and falls off the trolley.
If it is too far backwards the trolley will feel too heavy to lift at the front.
The position of the dinghy's equipment in the boat will affect the balance.
Move weight aft to lighten the load.

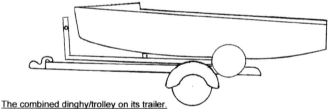

The combined dinghy/trolley on its trailer.
The trailer road wheels restrict the forward movement of the dinghy/trolley.
The centre of balance of the dinghy/trolley may be behind the road wheel pivot point.
There must be downward pressure at the towing hitch.
Move weight forward in the dinghy to trim for towing.

Launching trolley features.
Mainly lightweight aluminium.

Rear support fits hull, spreads load (timber).
Central rear roller for
ease of recovery.

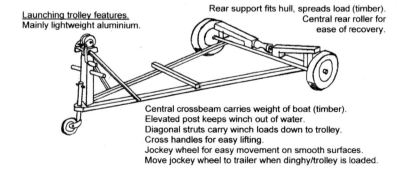

Central crossbeam carries weight of boat (timber).
Elevated post keeps winch out of water.
Diagonal struts carry winch loads down to trolley.
Cross handles for easy lifting.
Jockey wheel for easy movement on smooth surfaces.
Move jockey wheel to trailer when dinghy/trolley is loaded.

it, learning to lash it down, fix the trailer board, testing it, operating the hitch and all the other practical processes. Also in the story, you will see that I had to get him to tow it, as my car had no hitch. I sailed it for some years based in the dinghy park at my sailing club so I did not need a trailer, only a launching trolley. In this way, always sailing locally from my club, I practiced launch and recovery and the early stages of camping cruising.

Storage and Launching.
This is an issue to be addressed even before you acquire a boat. Where will you keep it and its trailer? Many sailing clubs do not like road trailers in dinghy parks. If they do allow them, they will probably charge for them. Is your garden or garage big enough? What would your alternatives be?

Some dinghy cruisers keep their boat at home on its trailer and head off to different locations to sail as their fancy and the current weather dictates. They find launching locations that suit them. These are important factors.
- The angle of the slip and its surface
- The cost of launching and recovery
- The availability, security and cost of parking for car and road trailer for the duration of the cruise.

Do not underestimate the physical effort required to engage in the loading / trailing / launching exercise. It will keep you fit.

Trolley / trailer.
As I did not have either of these I made them for myself. I am not recommending that you do this. I had no guidance at the time but since then I have seen a book called 'Boat trailers and tow vehicles. A users guide.' by Steve Henkel which has comprehensive information and does mention making your own trailer. A really good website to introduce newcomers to all aspects of towing, safety, legislation, vehicles and slipways is the Trail–Sail site (more details at the end of the book). I will outline some fundamentals that I discovered by undertaking the process.

Launching trolley.
- Needs to be as lightweight as possible as you will have to drag it, together with the boat's weight (often loaded) up sloping, slippery surfaces manually. (I used aluminium and timber with stainless fixings.)

- It needs to be as rust resistant as possible because it will be submerged frequently. (See materials just mentioned.)
- Pulling the loaded boat onto it in shallow water or even from the ground is a significant problem to be addressed. (I used a winch on the trolley.)
- The winch must be kept clear of the water.
- Getting it up/down steep ramps and roads/tracks, single handed to reach the trailer can be a problem. (I used a removable jockey wheel system, this allows the boat on its trolley to be **pushed** singlehanded uphill and steered from behind.) This is very important.
- Some additional ideas are:
- A system is needed for loading it onto the trailer and securing it there.
- The balance of the boat on the trolley must be correct. If the wheels are too far back in relation to the boat it will feel very heavy to lift at the bow. If the wheels are too far forward the boat will constantly be trying to tip off backwards.

Crossing shingle beach on trolley.

Road Trailer.

Must be of strong construction. All components may be purchased from a company called Indespension. (Details under 'Suppliers'.)

- It is a golden rule for me to NEVER submerge my road trailer in water. The corrosion risk to trailer and bearings is just not worth it. This may not be possible with bigger, heavier craft.
- It requires a jockey wheel. (I use the same one as on my launching trolley and move it back and forth between the two.)
- The balance with the boat loaded needs to be correct to give downward pressure on the towing hitch. This works in opposition to the loading requirement for the boat on the trolley. The trolley wheels when loaded do not come forward of the road trailer wheels. This can place the boat weight too far back on the road trailer causing it to tip up backwards. Movable weight in the boat will have to be trimmed forward to counteract this tendency.
- A trailer board, towing hitch and connections to the car are required.
- Spares and extras such as wheel, warning signs, light bulbs, jack, tools etc. will be needed (legally).

Launching strategies.

If a slipway is very slippery or steep, launch and recovery can be made easier by attaching the boat and trolley to the car's towing hitch with a long rope. The car is positioned on safer, flatter ground where the grip is good. Additional DCA information relating to this from David Platten 191/56. He uses a simple device commonly used in climbing called a 'Sticht plate' (a flat metal plate with a hole in it) to control the rope.

Recovery.

A more manual slower approach is to 'walk' the trolley with two chocks behind the wheels, sometimes called the 'two brick trick'. With the boat on the trolley facing up the slipway and a chock (brick) behind each wheel to stop it from running backwards, the trolley handle/jockey wheel is taken hard over to the left and the uphill wheel re-chocked. Now the handle is taken hard over to the right and the other wheel re-chocked. In this way it can be zigzagged up the incline. Margaret Dye has plenty of information and diagrams in her book about this and other methods.

A comprehensive 7 page DCA article 'At the End of the Trail' by Peter Bick covers heavier boat launch and recovery, trailers and equipment with precision and clarity in 127/14. Another detailed, updated outline is given by Alan Glanville 188/25

Maintenance.

For many sailors, 'Maintenance' means drudgery on an unprecedented scale. Maintenance is the reason for worshipping at the altars of plastics and stainless steel. For folks with newer craft in modern materials the maintenance load should be much reduced, but for older boats there is still the work to be done. Think of it like this. **Maintenance is 'Safety'.** Your safety. It's the boat's M.O.T. and you increase the risks to yourself if it is not done.

Much of the 'chore' of maintenance is in the mind. The cruising sailor can come to appreciate that it has its own peculiar attractions. If it is organised properly it can be as much a part of the experience of 'sailing' as handling the boat in a reaching breeze. It just needs the correct approach, and it needs to be appreciated that when cruising each skipper will be responsible for himself, his crew and craft and for getting them all back safely. The boat's gear is as important as the safety equipment carried by a climber up a rock face, it has to be reliable and much of this reliability will depend upon whether the equipment is well maintained.

There is a much-used phrase 'annual maintenance' which can be misleading. Yachting magazines tend to do 'Maintenance Specials' as winter progresses, for this is the traditional time for such activity and there is a general understanding that the summer is for sailing and the winter is for maintaining, but this need not necessarily be so.

A feeling of dissatisfaction should gradually overtake any sailor who leaves the boat untouched all winter intending to do some 'Spring Maintenance'. Throughout the winter there is the periodic nagging thought of 'I should be working on the boat.' and similarly, a string of valid reasons why this cannot be done, 'It's too cold/dark/wet etc.' Then, when that first unmistakable day of spring sunshine calls and the boat finally has to be worked on, it is found to be in a sorry state of neglect, with a mountain of maintenance to climb and it is still too cold for the best results when applying paint or varnish. To me, this seems to be one of the underlying reasons for some sailors to think of maintenance as a chore.

Constant Maintenance.

I have found that the best time for maintenance is NOW, that is, it is a continuous process and the word 'annual' simply means that this is the longest period that any single piece of gear should be left without major checking over. The greatest maintenance task is usually the repainting and re-varnishing of wooden components, especially the hull and deck on wooden boats. This should never be left until wintertime. It is best done in the middle of summer on a still, warm day when the washing off, rubbing down and varnishing can all be accomplished in quick succession with guaranteed, excellent results. Missing one day's sailing (when there is too little wind anyway) is no loss compared with the peace of mind at the end of the season when you know that there is nothing more to do, but wash the boat off and wrap it up. It is already prepared for the beginning of next season.

In the winter, of course, you can take home all the small portable bits and the one essential is to wash the salt off them. This is easy. After you have finished luxuriating in a nice deep bath of hot soapy water just take all the bits, especially ropes, blocks, etc and put them in to soak. Don't chuck the anchor in there, it chips the enamel, but it's still a good idea to dunk it and its warp into a bucket before losing it in the garage, otherwise you will have a mess of corroded chain to deal with next spring. After a good swish and a rinse with cold water, let them dry and put them away. Clean the bath before you are discovered. During the putting away process look everything over, in detail, searching especially for loose screws in wooden components and wear in small ropes. It is amazing what you find, especially with rudder and tiller assemblies. Remember. Put nothing away unless it is OK.

If you do your continuous maintenance for a couple of seasons you get to know your boat and its gear and you will find that a well maintained boat needs little 'maintenance'. When you see that your varnish has been chipped mid-season, dab some more on straight away. You don't have to wait until the appointed time to do it. Keep water away from wood. Doing it NOW stops further deterioration. It is safer, there are no guilty feelings over the winter period and you are safeguarding your investment.

Step-by step.

Remember what I advised back at the beginning about dividing the work into achievable 'bundles' so as not to get too downhearted. Don't pull everything to pieces. Do one thing at a time. You will need the intermittent rewards of seeing a shiny, new-looking re-assembled component and feeling the sense of achievement at its completion.

With the mobile cruising dinghy there is also the trolley/trailer system to keep up, as well as all the camping and domestic equipment. There is so much gear to be monitored that I usually try to keep a written note of anything that needs attention **as I am cruising,** then I check this upon my return and, of course, prior to going off on the next cruise. There is no disgrace in taking two or three seasons to gradually bring the boat up to standard, providing you do not compromise safety. One surefire way to lose interest is to wreck your boat in the garden or garage by removing everything, then find yourself unable to commit the time required and finally, gradually mislay many of the bits or forget which part goes where, because nothing is labeled.

Some tips.

- It is not necessary to strip whole objects (oars, floorboards etc.) right back to bare wood. Restoring patches will often do initially.
- Avoid using domestic Polyurethane varnish. It is very hard and cracks, then peels off in strips. It is difficult to sand damaged areas to a feathered edge. Marine varnish needs five coats from bare wood and the smoothness and shine is determined by the rubbing down between coats. Each layer will need several days (even a week) to become hard even in good weather. Dry varnish is not necessarily 'set' and 'cured' ie. set hard.
- It is quicker to remove small metal fittings than to try to work around them, but they must be kept and identified in a bag, tin lid, or box. The number removed at one time should be limited. No more than ten.
- We think of metals as being durable, but in a marine environment some of them deteriorate faster than wood especially anything that looks like 'brass'. Stainless steel reacts with aluminium and the two can get seized together, so be on the lookout, otherwise you may find castings such as deck cleats become impossible to remove. Double check metal bits.

7.

Cruising Tales.

DCA Quotes.

'I had not yet come to the end of my Utopia, I still had the marsh and the wildlife of the Medway to enjoy ... I lay gazing up at the heavens listening to the cries of the wildfowl that were flighting above me ... I was lulled to sleep by the contented cries of waders settling onto their roosts not far away.'

Peter Bick.

I SHOULD HAVE CAMPED ASHORE

7.
Cruising Tales.

I have written so much about the boat, its preparation and its systems that it is possible to forget what all this equipment is designed to do, namely, make it possible to set off on a cruise. The only cruises I have mentioned so far involved sailing with my family and forgetting my tent and pans as well as the 'fun' I had one windy night. The DCA bulletins have many accounts to be enjoyed. Wherever you might wish to sail, someone will have already cruised there and recorded their experiences for your education and enjoyment. A guide to their annual prize winning accounts called 'All that you've ever wanted to know about the Naylor Noggin' tells the story of the annual award for the best cruising account. The 'Noggin' is a tankard inscribed with the winners names. It is presented to each winner filled with a drink of his or her own choice. Brian Naylor began the tradition and it has been running for about 60 years. A similar DCA award is called Peter's Pint after Peter Bick and it is given to the member judged to have produced the best technical article. A talk given at the Annual General Meeting is known as the Peter Bick lecture.

For my conclusion, I will extract from two stories of my own single-handed sails to show just how different some cruising experiences can be from one another. The first, inland cruise 'In search of Charlie Allnut' is a bit of fun that poses an intriguing question. Where was I when I undertook this challenge? This story is actually just the introduction to a more lengthy account of the complete cruise, not published here, but available in the bulletin.

In Search of Charlie Allnut.

The sun was high in the sky and the heat becoming oppressive. The river twisted and turned through the narrow, verdant green valley hemmed in by the thick, lush foliage on either bank backed by impenetrable forest. I drifted on the current and the only sound was the hum of insects under overhanging tree branches on either side. I had seen nobody since yesterday when I had left the bustle of the isolated village behind me that gave access to these headwaters, to follow this silver track through the wild green wilderness. I had travelled long to reach the village and reached an agreement with the locals about launching my dinghy. I had checked my food supplies and especially my water for I knew that once I departed I would have to be self sufficient for several days. I had hoped to sail but no wind could penetrate down here below the thick leaf canopy of the trees and rowing became my only option.

There was an amazing variety of bird life all around me. My silent approach often startled them into flight from the deep reed beds or caused a defence action as the brightly coloured males flew off a short distance calling and creating disturbance whilst the duller females led their chicks through secret paths in the dense reed beds in the opposite direction. High, high above me I sometimes glimpsed big birds of prey circling on thermals constantly scanning for the weak and vulnerable below. Occasionally large varied flocks of birds gathered where grassland penetrated the forest and came down to the shore, their sentinels muttered low warning calls and all heads rotated slowly to observe my passing. Crested diving birds emerged from the depths shaking the fish that they had caught and most surprisingly seabirds (so many miles from the sea) systematically quartered the river behaving exactly like swallows as they hunted the fluorescent blue, green and red dragonflies that were everywhere. Fortunately the insects were not biting. I only took one hit as I crossed grassland ashore, returning to my boat after a short exploratory walk one evening. I had come prepared with various protective creams. This is not to say that the place was not without its dangers. Later, a snake was to swim with sinuous, smooth ability to within a few centimetres of me before disappearing into the reeds.

I rowed on, sweat dripping from me, stinging my eyes despite wearing a grimy sun hat dipped in the water. I covered legs and arms to avoid severe sunburn. Suddenly the boat lurched and slewed to the side. A cascade of twigs, leaves and bugs was cut from the tree branches overhead by the taught shroud wires as my stubby mast dragged through them. If only I could see where I was going. This is quite a problem when one is rowing day after day from early morning until the sun goes down in the evening. By midday the inside of the boat looked like the forest floor as it took too long to clear following each entanglement and after a time I just left it to be cleared at the end of the day. Travelling backwards meant sometimes almost getting the wrong side of islands where unseen dangers lay or running into reeds or shallows. On one occasion I snapped my rudder downhaul after getting into a shallow bay in this way. It was a good job I had everything on board to affect a repair. I had the rudder rigged whilst rowing and secured by the helm impeder. If I detected a small imbalance in my rowing, meaning I was consistently having to pull one oar harder than the other, I would give the rudder a gentle kick to correct it and keep the boat running on its most comfortable course.

There were animals in the grasslands. A herd came to investigate me when I had stepped ashore one evening to stretch my legs, unbend my aching back and rest my blistered hands. They were curious and edged closer and closer. Their eyes and mouths were the target of swarms of flies. Their muscular bulk was impressive and there was a constant loud sound of ripping grass as they fed as they approached. I stood my ground for a while but judged it safest to return to the boat when it looked like I might be surrounded. This wasn't the best time for a stampede, or even to have one stand on my foot. Sliding over the bank into the boat didn't allay all my apprehensions as they came to the very edge and looked down at me, sniffing my scent, with the ones at the back crowding the ones at the front. It would only take one casually placed foot, a slip or stumble and I would have half a ton of animal trying to share my 13 ft boat with me.

I did see people, but really most infrequently. On each occasion it was a surprise to both sides as one came across them suddenly, on rounding a bend, seeing a boat. I heard a woman's voice in the distance. I could tell what she was saying. She said, "That is different!" Then as she neared she called to me "You are the second one we have seen ..." There was a pause before she completed the sentence. " ... in four years." Yes, this was a unique experience. For the most part it was just me and the boat, the wildlife and the 'jungle' (how else can one describe it?) on either side. In seeking to convey the image to myself of what I was experiencing I could only think of Humphrey Bogart in the film 'African Queen'. The heat, the green, the effort, being in a boat, was all remarkably similar. He had a partner Rose Sayer (Katharine Hepburn). I was alone. He had an old steam engine. I had oars. He had leeches and he was called Charlie Allnut.

After four days of travelling I could tell from my map that I was nearing my destination. I began to search behind each island on the right hand bank for a narrow entrance onto a lake that I knew must be there somewhere. When I found it, it was blocked off and it looked like I could not get in. I wondered what to do as I drifted in the merciless sun. I rowed across to the opposite river shore to find forest shade whilst I formed a plan. I HAD to get around that blocked channel. I decided to re-cross the river, secure the boat *then clamber ashore and see what I could find. This I did. I stood looking at the lake, the grass and low bushes in the area. Which way to go? As I stood alone, a faint voice as if from nowhere called "Paul is that you?" Could it be Charlie Allnut? I turned to see the distant figure of my friend Dave walking towards me. "So glad you could make it." he said, "I've been keeping a lookout for you. Do you want a cup of tea?" Typically English I thought.*

The Location will be revealed later.

My own final tale completes this book in a similar way to which it began. It incorporates a number of questions. When we started, the early questions were all about what was needed to become a dinghy cruiser. Hopefully, as we have voyaged through the pages, some of the questions have been answered and an understanding has been reached. Do you have an affinity with the dinghy cruiser philosophy? Do you have a boat capable of becoming a cruising dinghy? Now that we are about to embark on sailing journeys, new questions arise, some of which are woven into the story of 'The Quaint Boat.' It tells of a short sail at sea. It mentions in passing a number of the normal, everyday decisions and process undertaken when cruising and it describes items of equipment that you may now be familiar with. It also illustrates some of the potential dangers involved and reflects on some sailing people's attitudes towards dinghy cruising. You will have to decide where you stand on the issues involved for yourself. This cruise account was fortunate to be awarded the 'Naylor Noggin', the premier award of the DCA, for the best cruise account for any given year.

This was an Autumn weekend cruise from Woodbridge at the head of the River Deben on England's east coast to meet up with the Royal Harwich Yacht Club's Wayfarer group cruise led by Anne and Dennis Kell (13 Wayfarers, 1 Wanderer.) in the Walton Backwaters, then return. No great excitement; just a weekend cruise.

The Quaint Boat.

I went sailing at the weekend. It's unusual for me to cruise the dinghy after the summer holidays have finished, but I was tempted out to meet up with some friends who were sailing to the Walton Backwaters from the River Orwell. I watched the weather forecasts all week. They were consistent. Ten knots northeasterly on Saturday with eight knots on the Sunday with warm sunshine. I couldn't miss it could I? My only problem was whether to wear my shorts and pack my jeans, or visa-versa. I launched onto a grey and silent Deben with a cold breeze chilling my knees. Perhaps it would brighten up later? I departed Woodbridge about 9.20 apparently the only person to be taking advantage of this dullish September weekend. The wind was up and down a bit. In the gusts I was glad I was on a dead run, with the full main. I would have needed a reef if I had been going the other way. Then the wind would die and I would have to be patient. I couldn't wait indefinitely as I had to be crossing the Bar at about 11.11 the time of Low Water. If the tide should gather momentum against me in the river I would be hard pushed to force my way out in my 13ft dinghy, even on the run. Above Waldringfield I secured the helm and started getting out my bigger headsail to rig it, but then the wind came up a bit and we began to move steadily. I waited a while, then stowed it away. I didn't really want to be carrying it out at sea. At 10.20 we were passing Ramsholt. At 11.05 I was going over the Bar having hove-to for a while just above the Horse buoy, to prepare for the sea sailing.

Visibility out there wasn't all that wonderful. It was grey, cold and a bit lumpy, but I was going at hull speed and enjoying the constant movement not often found goosewinging on a dead run. By 11.20 I was approaching Felixstowe pier and looking ahead to where various cruising yachts were sailing off the mouth of the Orwell. So ... there were other people about after all. The tide was going my way and the wind was getting stronger. Passing Landguard Point there were no big commercial craft in sight so I sped onwards across the shipping lane beginning to really enjoy the speed. She was surging on the waves and trying to surf. She is a relatively narrow craft compared with the Wayfarer style hulls. She is more akin to the GP14 and not designed to surf, - so I thought, but she began to skid along on the waves at times with the distinctive smooth motion of surfing and the rudder was starting to hum a bit, which I had not experienced in her before. Craft coming up the channel from Walton were not having an easy time. They pitched heavily as they powered into it; sailing cruisers with just a single sail set in a vain attempt to steady the boat. Their occupants were sheltering in their cockpits and looked at me with a mixture of surprise and wonder, as I suddenly appeared, that they should meet such a small boat in these uncomfortable waters. They weren't really smiling; they just had their teeth clenched.

At 12.20 I turned to port and hardened onto the wind a bit to shoot into the lee of Stone Point where the beach falls steeply into the water. I jumped out and held the boat. The place was deserted and I wondered if it had become a wildlife sanctuary. I was so used to seeing it covered with people, as it is a very popular place. I pulled her up and explored a little. I found faded footprints high on the beach that indicated that I was allowed to land. Within ten minutes along came a group of dinghies from Walton to land for lunch. After another ten minutes my friends from the Orwell began to arrive. Within half an hour things were back to normal.

After lunch I reefed and we sailed in company down Hamford Water and then followed Oakley Creek that is a favourite base for the local seals. There were quite a few around, on the beaches, on top of the saltings and in the water. Amongst the usual mixture of white, grey and black colours were some distinctly rusty red ones that were new to me. We sailed around a little and then started to make our way towards the marina. I usually try to avoid marinas, but with the number of boats and a plan to share an evening meal together, it was a sensible venue.

As soon as I entered the marina I was impressed by the noise. It was still quite windy and as it whistled through the rigging of hundreds of craft the sound generated was most disturbing. The incessant moaning of the rigging added to the banging of halliards, all trapped within the enclosed basin, created a doleful impression that ate into your consciousness as a dark and dismal background to all your thoughts. When you climbed the ramps up to the land surrounding the marina the sound died away, it was lighter, more pleasant and it was a relief to discover that there wasn't a gale force wind after all. Your cheerfulness returned on the tops of the banks only to be eroded as you descended into the moaning, dark and restricted confines of the basin bottom. It was a place to be avoided if at all possible.

After the evening meal, lying snug in my sleeping bag I had to block my ears, as it sounded as though the whole marina was being blown away around me. It did not feel good for the morning when I would have to retrace my steps to Woodbridge. I fell asleep working on a number of 'Plan Bs' in case sailing was impossible the next day.

Sunday dawned. The marina was still here. I hadn't been blown away and I wasn't drifting alone somewhere in the middle of the North Sea. The noise was slightly less, but still overwhelmingly depressive. I determined to reserve judgment about conditions until I had climbed the banks, where, in the blessed silence I found similar weather to the previous day except for a thinner cloud cover and the odd beam of sunlight showing through at times. My meteorological optimism of yesterday was replaced with realism and this time I wore the jeans and packed the shorts.

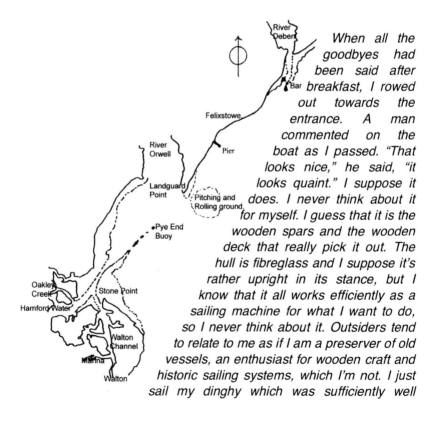

When all the goodbyes had been said after breakfast, I rowed out towards the entrance. A man commented on the boat as I passed. "That looks nice," he said, "it looks quaint." I suppose it does. I never think about it for myself. I guess that it is the wooden spars and the wooden deck that really pick it out. The hull is fibreglass and I suppose it's rather upright in its stance, but I know that it all works efficiently as a sailing machine for what I want to do, so I never think about it. Outsiders tend to relate to me as if I am a preserver of old vessels, an enthusiast for wooden craft and historic sailing systems, which I'm not. I just sail my dinghy which was sufficiently well made by its manufacturer that all its equipment continues to function after nearly forty years. I've had it so long, it now looks old fashioned and distinctive.

Outside it was blowing a gusty force-four-plus and the ebb was going against it. The Walton channel has twin rows of moored boats on either side of a narrow fairway, so singlehanding out of there was no easy ride. Only our group were sailing that day. People sat securely in their cruisers, pleased to be moored and enjoying the swirling ride, whilst we provided the entertainment. Our group was mainly Wayfarers, sailed two up and in these testing conditions the favourite rig was reefed main alone. Under this sail they sat up straight and maintained their speed whilst still being certain of their ability to tack. It was easy to see why they are so favoured for dinghy cruising. I set reefed main and jib on my Torch so I was a bit slow after tacking to get the headsail in and sheeted. I have a cover to extend my foredeck which is quite effective at returning solid water back overboard, but still I get a generous ration of spray coming inboard which adds to the stuff slopping up out of the centreboard case in rough beats such as this. I have a diaphragm bilge pump that I can rig on the thwart where it is accessible for me on either tack to pump the water, which gathers to leeward as I heel. As I cleared the moorings and approached Stone Point I tried it, only to find it was not sucking. I had to sort it out before I went to sea.

I landed on the beach and discovered that the end of the reinforced intake pipe had sheared where it was bent to enter the pump. I removed it, trimmed the damaged end, turned it end for end, then secured it and tested it. It worked. Good, I was going to need it when I emerged from the shelter of the land. I ate some food and watched the Wayfarers coming up. They only had to get to the Orwell. I had double that distance or more. At least the sun was shining now.

I was setting off an hour later than I should have been. I estimated a three-hour beat at sea with the favourable ebb. The target time on the Deben bar was 12.45 when the flood would start. Departing at 10.45 as I did would mean that the flood would begin to go against me by Landguard Point. However, I would be crossing the Rolling Ground and Pitching Ground areas off the point with no tidal flow and the water would be relatively smooth. I reckoned on beating for an extra hour at sea (four hours in all), to replace the time lost. The estimate proved to be accurate.

A final check that everything was in its proper place and I set off. The channel is like an extended slender funnel in shape with me at the narrow end. At the beginning it was very close tacking but as progress was made so the tacks could be extended and better progress made. There were some cruisers going out to return to the Orwell. They were trying to preserve a degree of comfort, restricting the heeling of their boats by shortening sail. They motored and used just the headsail to steady the craft. I assumed that this choice of sail was because it can be set and controlled without leaving the cockpit. In the rough water of the channel where the strongest tide was right against the wind I crossed tacks with them and as I had the maneuverability I sailed around them, keeping pace with their progress as they laboured up and over waves standing on their tails and then burying their bows. Their family crews had that same look of amazement mixed with some curiosity to see a recognisably vintage little boat out in the sea. They appeared to perceive great danger and extreme discomfort in their own situation. They all wore the accepted uniform of full designer oilskins, harnesses to clip them on and self-inflating lifejackets around the neck. I felt that their judgment of safety at sea was based upon this minimum standard. When the harness was attached to stainless steel fittings on a composite hull topped with Aluminium and Terylene they would be 'normal and secure'. Everything else that fell outside this standard they would need to think about and evaluate. Perhaps twenty or thirty years ago the smaller boat, the open boat, the timber and the gunter rig would have not have appeared so strange. Variety in boats was better understood and accepted then. People went to sea in what they had the skill to assemble, or with their restricted finances could afford to pull together for themselves, but today maybe things have changed? A cruiser now comes complete, with electrics, with upholstery, with plumbing, with security and a degree of isolation and protection from the elements provided by modern materials, current communications and reliable, powerful engines. A generation of family sailors is now at sea that has only known these standards.

As I approached the Pye End Buoy I noticed that it was the turning mark for the current cruising-racer fleet. They came powering in under their charcoal coloured laminated sails with their crews in neat rows along the windward rail squeezing every last little bit of efficiency from their muscular machines. They sat mutely gazing in my direction, no discussion, no smiles, no waving as in days gone by. They also seemed to be wrestling with their *impression of what they were seeing. Is that safe? Or, following on from that. Can you be safe at sea in a craft that doesn't have a liferaft in a canister, or being followed by a RIB (with an open VHF link) in close attendance?*

From the Pye End buoy I was able to hold close-hauled on the port tack and the sea state was much more comfortable when the wind and tide came together. Some small shelter from the land took the sting from the wind but began to limit my progress, yet still I had all the power I needed for most of the time. Roughly off the pier at Felixstowe I heard voices and looking around inshore I saw two Wayfarers using old Firefly sails slowly overhauling me on a similar course. They had a couple of teenagers aboard each. I could hear them laughing and enjoying themselves. As they closed with me they shouted across to know where I was going. They were going to Felixstowe Ferry they said as they went by. They had been camping down at the same marina as me overnight and I had heard that they were on their Duke of Edinburgh Award expedition. Now they were on their way back. It was my turn to wonder. Just kids, out here. They were sailing well and looking out for each other. They were based at the Ferry Sailing Club and quite used to sailing on the Deben bar. Anyone who knows will tell you it is a scary place to sail. It makes good sailors. Thanks to their enlightened instructors the youth of today can still access adventure.

They sailed more off the wind than I did and put in a few tacks whilst I held the single tack until approaching the entrance. I followed their inshore tack and was disappointed to find reduced wind close to the beach. I toyed with the idea of going to full main, but I knew that the wind would be funneled against me as I tried to get into the river mouth and so I crept along with my reef in. With several short tacks I maneuvered in towards the starboard Bar buoy and then began tacking for the port mark which seems to sit right on the bar itself. Away from shelter the wind was up and the roar of the waves breaking on the shingle was rising. The turbulent water was still against me until I could get further in but it was getting so narrow that I was obliged to push the tacks beyond the limits of the channel just to gather sufficient way to make progress. I made it to the port mark and felt that from this point I would be entering the influence of the water being sucked into the river. I approached the narrowest section inside the highest shingle bank on the bar. As an observer, this is where you see the greatest danger for there was hardly room to tack my little dinghy, but far worse was yet to come.

After this narrow nip, the bar on my right hand side became flatter and broader. Although the water was shallow over it, the incoming waves from the sea were driving right across the top of it. It was almost as if the bar wasn't there. There was no protection. To the left was the steeply banked shoreline running straight for half a mile or more to the gap where the river exits the land. The deep channel followed it and was within metres of it. The width of the usable sailing water hardly stretched to tens of metres. The waves crossing the course to be sailed were being driven onto this lee shore where they exploded and were reflected back to collide with the next incoming waves. To enter the river meant beating along this narrow corridor of breaking waves and surf trying to judge the very final moment when to tack to maximize progress by keeping up boat speed. The port tack out towards the incoming waves rapidly lifted the bow in an explosion of spray and solid roaring water and almost halted progress; all the time heading for the whitewater, swirling shallows that indicated the solid mass of unyielding pebbles of the bar laying in wait, inches below the surface. How far could one go before hitting it? The starboard tack was virtually right at the shore. The incoming wave lifted the boat and drove her towards it so that destruction seemed inevitable. To miss the tack in this situation would have seen the boat crunch onto the shingle and be rolled out and down by the backwash, only to be swamped within seconds as the next roller came in to pound her into matchwood instantly. I was caught out on the second tack at this point, simply by the scend of the wave. I had made the tack and she was turning outwards, but as the wave crashed against the shore, so the water level was dropped and the boat sank into the trough. The centreboard hit the bottom with enough force to snap its restraining elastic that shot like a broken rubber band up into the bow of the boat. I grabbed the half-up board and whacked it down again praying that it was still intact below the boat.

The worst was over after about two hundred metres in this maelstrom for the channel broadened sufficiently for a decent tack and the tidal stream increased in strength and became more favourable in direction. The wind was strong and I was pleased with my earlier decision to stay reefed. I was joyous that my boat had seen me through as the tide sped me into the river. I only had the six-mile length of the Deben left to tack up.

Above the Horse buoy I sailed lazily whilst getting some food and drink and pumping out the boat. As Ramsholt came into sight I sheeted in again and brought her hard on the wind. The river was full of boats on moorings. A few sailing cruisers motored; one or two went gently in the opposite direction under reefed headsail. Here was a riverful of sailing potential. Here were millions of pounds worth of dedicated equipment waiting to be used. The number of craft that I had seen out and about in these two days was insignificant beside the numbers that were garaged on their moorings and secured in marinas. I was reminded of the first chapter of Charles Stock's book 'Sailing Just for Fun' *in which he makes the case for the small cruiser.*

'The boats I meet around the coast seem to be bigger each season. .... but do they give more and better sailing? I think not.
... it seems to me that there must be some correlation between the size of the boat and the time available to sail her.

We must have a life support system, but it can be a capsule rather than a caravan.'

Above Ramsholt I drifted in the channel whilst I shook out the reef. Above Waldringfield in the shelter of the land it was perfect gentle sailing in the evening sunshine on empty water. The forecasted eight knots of wind had finally arrived. Charles Stock also says **'Many of us ... want some sort of challenge when we go afloat.'.** *This was the perfect fulfillment of my weekend's challenge.*

A couple of dinghies sailed at Woodbridge. One landed on the slipway at the same time as me and its owner kindly helped me pull up my trolley. "Have you just been out for a couple of hours?" *he asked.* "No I went out yesterday. I've been down to Walton and back." *His face went blank. He stepped back and looked at the boat.* "In that?" *he said almost involuntarily. I smiled.* "It's quaint isn't it?"

Read Charles Stock's final cruise. Swallowing the Anchor 211/61.

Location? Location? Location?

There is still that loose end to tie up concerning my river voyage. Snakes in the water, 'eagles' (and later, flocks of green parakeets) in the sky, with the 'jungle' all around me. Where was I?

In Search of Charlie Allnut.

Conclusion.

I had arrived at the Dinghy Cruising Association gathering at the Beale Park, Thames Boat Show near Pangbourne after rowing sixty miles down the River Thames from Lechlade in a swelteringly, sunny June. The higher reaches of the river are deeply rural and in places give the impression of pristine 'wilderness'. This is in large part due to the efforts of the Environment Agency that is in charge of maintaining the river. To me it was a great and much appreciated surprise and I have sought to spring a similar surprise upon you, the reader, in an effort to make you appreciate what interesting exploration and adventure lies within your grasp by taking simple practical steps towards finding it. I was so impressed by the river journey that I returned later in the year to complete well over a hundred miles of the non-tidal Thames by oar and sail, meeting many interesting people and seeing wonderful sights throughout. I completed the tidal journey to Southend later, but that's another story. Yes, you guessed, it's in the DCA bulletin, now called 'Dinghy Cruising'

My little boat has carried me to these and to many other enjoyable experiences. One of my seasons took in sea sailing in Kircudbright, Scotland, then Lake Coniston in England's Lake District followed by Holy Island and Lindisfarne (see front cover) in the north east of England from Woodbridge in Suffolk. What other kind of cruiser has such flexibility of venues in a season's sailing? I can take my little sailing home with me when I visit other countries. There are little boats doing similar things for other people. Will you be in one of them? Who knows? Perhaps we will meet on the water? Perhaps I might read your story, see your 'snapshots' in the DCA bulletin?

There's a description of how to contribute in 194/06.

Final words from the DCA. A super, poetic 'snapshot'.

Bill Bailey in Camusfearna. The Bay of Alders. 127/10.
17ft Inflatable Catamaran.

The croft white under the trees, the curve of the beach, the stream bubbling down. The half tide pools and the green islets. Almost breathing, waiting for someone to come. "I'd like to stay ... we don't really have to go." A wide turf ledge, birch and rowan flanked, with mossy rocks around. "This will do fine – we'll pitch just here."

Views down the beach, down the long sound. The meadow behind and the quiet croft beyond. Ears pricked for an otter's mew. We read, explore the pools, gather driftwood for the smoky fire. The tide drops down while feeding seabirds call. Dry now the boat sits safe and our islands grow and change. "Look at these mussels ...look at the size." A grey great heron stares from his rock in the creek. A pot bubbling on the fire, flames flicker in the glade. Shadows gather under early stars while a marsh bird pipes along the shore. " Can we do this again some day?"

Here is a land best found from the sea.
Light and shade and shadow.
Bright days and sombre, birdsong and green meadows.
Travellers find some of themselves here and so did we.

8.

Finally.

DCA Quotes.

'As night fell, my little candle lantern swung gently from the boom whilst the boat rocked me to sleep and above me my masthead light slowly wandered around amongst the stars.'
David Sumner.

Practical Dinghy Cruiser

Contacts.

The search for any general information can begin here.

The DCA. <u>www.dinghycruising.org.uk</u>
Informed, friendly, only minimally organised, an Association for individuals who meet from time to time, before going their own ways again.' **Joan Abrams.**

Royal Yachting Association.

<u>www.rya.org.uk</u>

email. <u>admin@rya.org.uk</u>

RYA House. Ensign Way,

Hamble, Southampton SO31 4YA.

Tel. 0845 345 0400

Coastguards. (Coastguard Form CG6 and Small Ships Register.)

<u>www.mcga.gov.uk</u> email. <u>infoline@mcga.gov.uk</u>

The Maritime and Coastguard Agency

Spring Place, 105, Commercial Road,

Southampton. Hampshire SO15 1EG

Tel. 023 8032 9100

Lifeboat.

<u>www.rnli.org.uk</u>   email <u>info@rnli.org.uk</u>

Royal National Lifeboat Institution.

West Quay Road, Poole,

Dorset. BH15 1HZ.   Tel. 0845 122 6999

Suppliers.
Electric Power.
www.electric-boat-association.org.uk
Electric Boat News.
150, Wayside Green,
Woodcote
Nr. Reading,
Berkshire. RG8 0QJ
Tel. 01491 681449
secretary@eboat.org.uk

Field & Trek.
Camping equipment.
8-9 Grays Brewery Yard
Springfield,
Chelmsford.
www.fieldandtrek.com
(Technical guide.)
Tel 01245 283999

Point North. (Items for tents)
Porthdafarch Road,
Porth Dafarch,
Holyhead, Anglesey
Gwynnedd. LL65 2LP
www.profabrics.co.uk
Tel. 01407 760195
Fax. 01407 763049
Email info@profabrics.co.uk

Moonshine Publications.
(Publishers of this book
and with others in the
pipeline.) See details on
inside pages at front and
'Seasickness' (below).

PennineOutdoor.
(Items for tents)
Central Buildings
Main Street,
High Bentham
N. Yorkshire.
Lancaster LA2 7HE

www.pennineoutdoor.co.uk
Tel. 015242 63377
Tel. 015242 63377

Trailers.
(Everything required.)
www.indespension.co.uk
Tel 01204 478500

www.trail-sail.org.uk
(A very, very useful site
with good information.)
Vehicles.
Slipways
Legislation.

Practical Cruiser Guide

Seasickness

Designs.
Explorer. (184/17. 185/73, 188/36)
www.mitchellyachts.co.uk
E-mail. mukti@mitchellyachts.co.uk
Mitchell Yachts Ltd.
Rat's Castle. Clovelly,
Bideford   Devon EX39 5TF
Low Carbon.
www.resurgence.org/ carbon calculator

Paradox (181/36, 193/45 for 'User report.')
www.microcruising. com. Apart from boat designs this website has a fascinating list of 'epic' voyages in small boats from 1789 to 2001, including transatlantic trips in boats as small as the 5' – 4" long 'Fathers Day' (Don't try this at home!) in 1993.
A UK Paradox builder Alastair Law has photographs of complete construction and also sailing details of 'Little Jim' (illustrated in this book). Contact through the DCA.

Topper Cruz Forum. www.groups.yahoo.com/group/toppercruz.

Launching.
There are a number of books on the subject usually called 'Where to launch…' There are inland waterways and lake versions. Mine is called 'Where to launch around the coast.' by Diana van der Klugt. (Opus book publishing.) If this title is put into a book supply website like www.amazon.co.uk it will produce a range of titles.
Another site is www.boatlaunch.co.uk

General Interest.
Use a search engine and look for 'small sailboats'. Comprehensive lists of contacts for 'suppliers' of all manner of small boats, forums constructors, news, outline plans, cruise accounts, books, etc. Warning. Once you start, it's endless, make sure you have the time!

Seasickness. Practical Cruiser Guide. Cover by Mike Peyton.
Another Moonshine publication. ISBN 978-0-9572161-0-5 contains the information that people have long searched for. The latest scientific findings, not previously brought together. It offers helpful advice and a range of practical strategies to minimize the effects, based on **understanding** what is happening. See the website.

Books.

Having mentioned above where you might buy them I have to remind you of the DCA library resources that are 'encyclopedic'. Why go anywhere else?

The full list can be obtained from the librarian but I can give just the glimmer of an idea here. There are different categories available.

Dinghy cruising. Camping & Living aboard. About 50 titles.

Dinghy Sailing. Racing, Rigs, sails and techniques. About 40.

Seamanship. Boat handling, Navigation, Safety, Tides and Meteorology. About 60 titles.

Boat Types/Classes, Equipment, Trailers,

Engines and Electrics.

About 20 books and about 40 manufacturer's data sheets.

Boat building and Design. Plans, Modifications, Repair and Maintenance. About 40 titles and four sets of plans.

Canoeing, Inflatables and Underwater. About 18 titles.

Lakes, River and Inland Waterways. About 20 titles.

Pilots, Guides, Cruising Areas, Charts and launching Sites.

About 50 pilotage. About 30 sets of charts.

Some overseas pilotage books.

Voyages, Cruises, Travel and Biographical.

About 100 titles plus many Roving Commissions from the RCC.

Maritime History, Shipbuilding and Fishing Industry.

About 25 titles.

Humour, Fiction and Children's Books. About 15 titles.

Sailing and Cruising General, Miscellaneous.

About 60 titles plus blocks of specialist magazines.

Some boats covered in DCA Bulletins.

It is impossible to include all the information here about every class of boat so this is just a selection of named classes with some early references (restricted by column width). The actual list has the up to date references and **many more craft can be found**.

Albacore 8/7, 20/11, 21/10, 82/12
Bosun 24/2, 26/2
Catapult Cat 127/8, 137/24
Cruz 147/24, 148/13, 165/46
Devon Dayboat 103/9, 103/14
Dockrell 72/13, 111/8
Drascombe Dabber 80/11, 87/8
Drascombe Lugger 44/4, 61/8, 93/14
Express Pirate 124/10, 146/19
Finn 141/27
GP 14. 116/23, 129/29, 139/29
Graduate 73/4, 149/17
Highlander 14. 166/24, 169/42
Javelin 90/10
Laser Stratos 170/55
Loch Broom P. Boat 137/19, 181/30
Mayfly 14/2, 22/3, 87/25, 105/15
Midshipman 12/5, 72/16
Mirror 16. 133/22, 137/28, 184/41
National 12 185/52
Nimrod 150/12
Outrigger Canoe 185/64
Pelican 168/41
Rebell 46/9, 49/10, 157/30
Roamer 58/8, 59/11, 112/18
Salcombe Yawl 44/6,98/8
Seafly 139/27
Shearwater Cat 116/12, 144/17
Skipper 17. 139/15, 150/18, 151/34
Suffolk Beach Punt 168/29
Swampscott Dory 149/22, 164/38
Tideway 46B/7, 85/14,
Torch 97/6, 109/12, 149/14, 163/35
Vagabond 102/18, 127/11
Wayfarer 33/5, 39/12, 61/9, 92/11
Westray 16. 149/29, 156/20, 165/29

Beaufort 141/17, 147/27,
Cadet 133/13, 142/13
Cormorant 105/22, 138/21,
Dabchick 130/31
Devon Yawl 136/17
Dragonfly 148/23
Drascombe Lgboat 62/10,
Explorer 184/17, 185/73
Falcon 19/5, 29/5, 75/13,
Firefly 4/3, 134/31
Gull 47/7, 134/13
Heron 43, 80/16, 90/9
Hitia Cat 181/27, 183/25
Kestrel 111/24, 117/22,
Leader 135/12, 138/11,
Lune Whammel 129/15
Merlin Rocket 38/4
Mirror 11. 65/9, 78/13,
Morag 91/20
Ness Yawl 150/36, 165/34
Otter 88/15, 181/42
Paradox 181/36
Privateer 145/21
RNSA 14. 180/8
Sailfish 65/4
Sandpiper 152/19
Seagull 154/31
Skipper 14. 86/11
Solent Seagull 4/14
Sunspot 49/9,156/19
Tarpon 76/12
Tiki Cat 131/14
Tricorn 14/2, 54/5, 72/15
Wanderer 89/8, 91/13,
Wavecrest 27/9, 32/2
West Wight Potter 42/6,

New Boats?

Reluctant as I've been to name a newer, modern boat, if I am pressed, I would suggest that a visit to www.swallowboats.com should point you in the right direction. You will also find the latest trends being discussed and evaluated on Small Craft Advisor. www.smallcraftadvisor.com.

Conversion of dimensions.

I have quoted many Imperial dimensions because the boats concerned were first specified in these sizes and even European craft are often still classified in Imperial lengths today.

For anyone wishing to approximate linear dimensions rapidly.

25mm = About an inch.   300mm = About a foot.

1 metre = About 3 feet (a yard)

For greater precision.

Inch to millimeter (multiply by 25.4)

Millimetre to inch (multiply by .0394)

Feet to metre (x .3048) Metre to feet. (x 3.2808)

Fathoms – metres (x1.8288)   Metres-Fathoms (x .5468)

Weight Conversion.

14 (lbs) pounds = 1 stone.

2.2 lbs = 1 Kilogram. I Kilogram = 1,000 grams

1 Cub. metre of buoyancy (about 35 cub ft) supports 1 Tonne.

Area.

Sq. ins to sq. mm   (x 645.16)   Sq. mm to sq. ins. (x .00155)

Sq. ft. to sq. meters (x   .0929)   Sq. metres to sq. ft (x 10.76)

Notice these last figures that allow sail area in square feet to be very roughly converted into square metres by dividing by 10 (and vice-versa)

The Torch story.

Bert Keeble and his wife Linda came to meet me in Woodbridge in May 1998. During this visit the following information was gathered by discussion and later from a copy of a letter from Derrick Cobden.

Bert Keeble was raised in Maldon. His dad and his father before him were barge skippers, so it could be said that salt water ran in the veins of the family. It is a little surprising to learn therefore that Bert served his time in the electronics trade at Marconi's in Chelmsford. Bert assures us that we can forget his early designs for a combined television, record player and radio which was the size of a sideboard and concentrate on boats, that's what he did.

He recalls one of his typical early sailing projects, just after the war, was an old ship's lifeboat that he bought for five pounds (and that included the Wellington boots). The hull (that's all there was of it) was lying grounded and full of mud on the shores of Northey Island in the Blackwater. His first task was to shovel the mud out and get it to float again long enough to reach an accessible boatyard before it sank.

In the fifties he was dabbling with canoes and little boats of all types, as well as helping others to learn to sail mainly through the Central Council for Physical Recreation. About this time he taught at Maldon Grammar School before transferring to run a sailing centre at Heybridge based on the old barge yacht 'Mamgu' and here a close friend, Derrick Cobden takes up the story.

'In the middle fifties an interest was being taken in school sailing by Hertfordshire Education Committee who set up a sailing centre at Barton Broad in Norfolk under the auspices of the Hertfordshire Education Foundation. This enabled schools that had a person with an inclination towards sailing, to take a party for one week. A system was evolved where the coach taking the outgoing school up would return the previous school party. This became a popular outing and it was soon realised that for it to continue it was necessary for staff to be trained. Each Easter a staff course was arranged and Bert was invited to assist with instructing by Eric Howells. During one of these courses discussions took place as to the suitability of boats for teaching and for the use of young people. At that time any type of craft was used for instruction and the Barton centre had a very mixed bag. It was felt that a 13ft dinghy with room for an instructor and two pupils would be desirable but one of *that description, that was a reasonably stable machine, was not to be found. At that time the Enterprise had been born but it was felt that even with a reduced rig it didn't quite fit the bill.*

Ideas and requirements were formulated ie. 13 ft long, stable, could be built in schools, low cost, reasonable performance. It was suggested that Bert should design it. During the winter he prepared the plans and presented them to Ben Dunn the PE Educational Organiser who agreed to finance it at a (remembered) cost of £60. Derrick had met Bert about eighteen months previously and they had cooperated on several small projects. Derrick worked at the Cheshunt County secondary school where the very enthusiastic headmaster Frank Smith gave permission for Derrick to build the prototype in the school workshop out of school time. Bert then made the frames and took them to the school. During a period of about six weeks Bert visited each weekend Saturday and Sunday, to approve Derrick's ongoing work and to assist in completing the building in time for the Easter Course. The boat was named 'HEFOD' after the name of the foundation (and One Design). What was to become known as the first Torch dinghy had a brilliant send off. It was launched at the Cheshunt Pit by Sir William Ackland.

Originally all the fittings were hand made and tinned (Bert was a metalwork teacher) though this was discovered not to be a good idea. The sails came from a firm in Brightlingsea; the plywood was a good exterior grade. The original dinghies had steel centreplates but these were soon discarded for wooden ones.'

Bert tried to make the design as practical and as versatile as possible. He had a long association with Sea Scouts and had run courses for them based at Woolverstone Hall (now Ipswich High School for Girls) near Pin Mill on the River Orwell in Suffolk. The boats used for the courses were whalers loaned from HMS Ganges at Shotley further down the Orwell. The boats had to be collected and then rowed up to Woolverstone. Rowing was an essential part of what was learned in boat handling in those days and this explains one of the distinct design features of the Torch.

There are two oarlock positions, one being well forward of the normally placed set, just astern of the thwart. The shortened foredeck allows sufficient space for someone to sit on top of the forward buoyancy tank to use the forward oarlock position. This unusual cutout foredeck has the very useful property of creating more room inside the boat, as one crewperson (or two small children) can occupy this space when sailing and not interfere with the running of the craft.

Bert Keeble boat designer. Torch 269.

By the standards of similar sized craft the Torch has a deep and relatively narrow hull form. This makes it easy to row with 'normal' sized oars. Its modest sail area means that usually it can be comfortably sailed from within the boat rather than having to sit the boat out. Although some of the Torches have had toe straps, they are not really required and this has the further advantage of freeing space inside the boat to allow ease of movement for the crew. Small sidedecks. extend right around the boat with a raised coaming to keep the splashes of spray where they should be.

The narrow hull has a distinct advantage in extremely light airs as the boat continues to ghost along when others with broader beams and flatter bottoms start to struggle. Although the upright style of the Torch does not conjure up visions of speed in the observer it will be found that a well-sailed Torch is not a slouch. Another special quality, maybe a unique ability, of the boat can be found if it necessary to roll it onto its side on land, to access the underside or the centreboard fixing. With a stripped out boat one strongish man can manage this alone and the boat will stand on its edge due to its fairly upright topsides. It can be secured in this position by putting a little weight on the masthead if it is rigged, or by chocking the tiller underneath the moulded keel strip near to the centerboard slot.

All the early Torches had a sliding-gunter rig and nothing complex in the gear. There was no gooseneck, only a crutch on the end of the boom. No rigging screws only lanyards. No sail slides to feed into no track. No halliard exit sheaves to catch the rope/wire halliard splice. These sophistications were replaced with pure simplicity. Most modern sailors are amazed to meet such elementary systems; they can't believe that just wood and rope can make so much expensive stainless steel redundant.

Bert Keeble later moved to Cowes on the Isle of Wight where he was the principal of the National Sailing Centre.

Bert died 21 November 2008.

The Torch Design.

Bert also designed a small cruiser, which he called 'Flambeau', which is French for the same symbol.

The original Torch was specified as:
L.O.A 13ft. Beam 5' - 1". Sailing Weight 248lbs
Built in Buoyancy 600lbs
Sail Area. Main 62 sq ft. Jib 18 sq ft.
Original kit price £83-4-0
Ready to sail £148
At educational sailing centres where they were very heavily used they led a knockabout life. They were often sold off at cheap prices (Around £250 when this one was bought). In some places they continue to be used and sold in this way.

Their Names.
As they were used in fleets they often had 'linked' names ie. they were named after identifiable groups such as 'Seabirds' or Snow White's 'Dwarves'. My particular Torch 269 came from Suffolk where 'Sea Areas' ie, Viking, Forties, Bailey and Biscay were used. It is pure chance that it was called 'Tyne' and my name is Constantine (*'Constant Tyne'* is a name that has been written on the boat in the past). It was one of the first boats to be sailed by me (when learning to sail) at Oulton Broad in 1963 when it was relatively new. This makes it quite an old lady.

Some Characteristics.

Teaching in the Torch.

By current fashion the boat looks a little narrow, but it has deep sides and under most circumstances it can be sailed without sitting it out. This is an important cruising comfort consideration as one is IN the boat rather than ON it and this affords a degree of weather protection. In tuition situations it immediately gives novice sailors a feeling of confidence, releasing them from the initial fear of the possibility of instant capsize. It allows them to relax and appreciate the feeling of sailing and to concentrate on learning how to do it. When the pupils improve, the instructor can sit on the forward buoyancy tank, forward of the mast, looking astern. This allows pupils to experience the true feeling of managing the boat by themselves, by 'removing' their tutor who is, nevertheless, still able to monitor their progress by watching the expressions on their faces as they react to the developing circumstances ahead of the boat, behind his/her head. It is perceived as a mark of the instructor's confidence in the ability of the pupils, when the instructor is prepared to release the sailing responsibility to them in this way. Many sailors have benefited from learning their sailing in the Torch and all have appreciative memories of their time in this little boat.

Optimum balance of craft requirements?

A cruising dinghy which is not too heavy for a single person to launch, sail and recover singlehanded, without recourse to special additional equipment can be a more manageable, more mobile unit. All craft involve some kind of compromise whatever their purpose. Whilst the boat is not 'fast' it is not very slow either, particularly when only carrying one adult. Smaller craft are lighter, but can become cramped for space; larger craft may have the room but become heavier and more expensive. The secondhand Torch comes close to providing the optimum balance of space and weight requirements for dinghy cruising and it is a very affordable solution.

Saving the Best 'til Last.

For anyone who has read every word until this point, here is your reward. Throughout the book there have been numerous references to the extracts taken from the DCA Bulletin and it may be that you have wished and wondered how you could access these and other works contained in the first 50 years of the publications.

Well, you can.

Here are the last references for you 207/22.

The CD of the first 50 years of the bulletin will be made available to members to purchase. (*The CD is designed for PCs with Windows and Word.* The CD is amazingly cheap. The list of 'Contents' of the bulletins now runs well over 100, A4 pages.

To make this incredible amount of information available took years of work by dedicated members, as explained in a letter 207/29. **Doug Forster** *(Librarian) collated, assembled, put in the 3000 or so hyperlinks from the index to the articles one by one then tested them all.* **Alan Barker** *scanned all the other 1000 articles mentioned in the index, corrected the index, put Mike Williams and John Hughes' scans into common format and redrew lots of diagrams to make them screen friendly. Based on work and assisted by, Joan Abrams, Keith Muscott, Liz Baker, Len Wingfield.*

Wow!
Here is that key to the world of dinghy cruising mentioned on the back cover.

You can get half a century's worth of experience of dinghy cruising on a **CD**, for about the same basic cost as this book, from the DCA.

The library now has 'Loan CDs' for every issue since the year 2007 and the editor will look sympathetically on requests for specific articles and images, or even full bulletins from 2007 up to the present day. You need not miss a single word, picture or diagram.

What are you waiting for? Happy reading.